JAMARR'S PROMISE

Mom

Thank you for never clipping my wings and always letting me soar. For not only teaching but truly showing me the true meaning of unconditional love.

Even in your death, you have taught me one of the greatest lessons of life: success cannot be measured in the money that you make but in the lives that you have touched along the way.

"But whatever road you choose, I'm right behind you win or lose"

—Rod Stewart

JAMARR'S PROMISE

A True Story of Corruption, Courage, and Child Welfare

**Kristin I. Morris and
Joseph J. Zielinski, Ph.D.**

JAMARR'S PROMISE

This book is designed to provide accurate and authoritative information
with regard to the subject matter covered. This information is given with the
understanding that neither the author nor Wisdom House Books, Inc.
is engaged in rendering legal, professional advice.

The opinions expressed by the author are not necessarily those
of Wisdom House Books, Inc.

Published by Wisdom House Books, Inc.
Chapel Hill, North Carolina 27514 USA
1.919.883.4669 | www.wisdomhousebooks.com

www.jamarrspromise.com

Wisdom House Books is committed to excellence
in the publishing industry.

Book design copyright © 2017 by Wisdom House Books, Inc.
All rights reserved.

Cover and Interior design by Ted Ruybal
Edited by Arielle Hebert

Published in the United States of America

Hardback ISBN: 978-0-9983799-1-3
Paperback ISBN: 978-0-9983799-0-6
Ebook ISBN: 978-0-9983799-2-0

LCCN: 2017933033

FAM001010 FAMILY & RELATIONSHIPS / Abuse / Child Abuse
POL019000 POLITICAL SCIENCE / Public Policy / Social Services & Welfare
BIO026000 BIOGRAPHY & AUTOBIOGRAPHY / Personal Memoirs

First Edition
14 13 12 11 10 / 10 9 8 7 6 5 4 3 2 1

Table of Contents

Acknowledgments

I thank my husband Benny and our children for standing beside me during this lengthy ordeal. I thank my father and mother, my step-mother Maria, my brothers Jimmy and Christopher, my sister Kerri, and my sister-in-law Noreen, for their help and support. All of these people made my efforts possible and meaningful. I will never forget Jamarr, the nine-year-old boy who was murdered after I was removed as his caseworker, and I dedicate this book to him. Most of all, thanks to those who have expressed their willingness to testify in any legal proceeding directed at seeking justice for Jamarr Cruz and myself.

—Kristin I. Morris

I thank my wife Patti for her love and support throughout this entire endeavor. I thank Karen Whirledge, my office manager, for her diligent work all of these years. And finally, I thank Kristin for the opportunity and honor to know and share with her the real life events depicted in this memoir. She did the right thing…and she has paid the price for it.

—Joseph J. Zielinski, Ph.D.

Preface

The New Jersey Division of Youth and Family Service (DYFS), renamed the Division of Child Protection and Permanency (DCPP) in 2012, has a checkered and troubled history in the state. This state agency is dedicated to the protection of abused and neglected children and the provision of services to their families with a goal of family preservation. A number of reportedly preventable child deaths have been in the local news over the years. The division's ongoing difficulties culminated in the shocking revelation of the four Jackson boys, who were found emaciated and eating out of garbage cans in Collingswood, NJ while in their adoptive home. It appeared that they were being systematically starved while they were under DYFS's care.

As a result of the Jackson case, and earlier tragedies, Marcia Robinson Lowry, a renowned child advocate attorney and then Executive Director of Children's Rights, spearheaded a lawsuit against the state, originally filed in 1999. The caseworkers' union, the Communications Workers of America, applauded the lawsuit which, among other things, set limits on caseload sizes and led to the hiring of more caseworkers. New Jersey's Attorney General's Office threw up a series of legal roadblocks, which they eventually removed. In 2003, this resulted in Federal oversight over the division and the placement of a

Federal Monitor, Judith Meltzer. The monitor's job was to supervise the agency's pursuit of rectifying over fifty identified deficiencies in the service delivery system.

Parenthetically, a billion dollars has been spent since 2003 when combining Federal and state funds to improve the division's service delivery within the State. DCPP was to develop, among other things, a data driven approach to case management, to make case decisions more objective and less open to subjective influences. Early on, low level supervisors and rank and file employees became concerned that the division's administration was attempting to hurry up to simply "check the boxes" to meet the deficiencies, rather than making real changes, a claim disputed by the administration.

The citizens of New Jersey are disinterested in DCPP at best, and opinions are generally negative when asked for. They believe that the division oversteps its authority on some child cases, or doesn't do enough to protect the most vulnerable children in other situations.

The series of lawsuits against DYFS/DCPP have spanned six governorships. The timeline of events that follow in this memoir span two governorships: the single term of Jon Corzine and the two terms of Chris Christie. Due to DCPP having met about twenty-one of fifty-three of its designated goals, and having partially met ten others, on November 4, 2015, Governor Christie made a Sustainability and Exit Plan to have the Federal oversight of DCPP lifted. The wisdom of this is questionable. When personal gain, vested interests, self-aggrandizement, and cronyism operate, the results are disastrous, even when a veritable fortune has been spent to help the situation and even among the most laudable intentions.

This book is about my journey as a caseworker through this socio-political morass. It is an attempt to shed light on unprofessional decisions influenced by personal beliefs at variance with sound professional practice. The aim is to protect innocent children from the sad and totally unnecessary fate of Jamarr Cruz.

The names of the main characters are true, with the exception of my other cases, my confidant, select coworkers, and the two women pressured to alter their testimony.

Jamaar Cruz Vigil from the Courier-Post.

Photo by Jose Moreno, courierpostonline.com.
Copyright by the Courier-Post. Used with permission. All rights reserved.

Chapter 1

The suburban New Jersey town of Pennsauken changed a lot in recent years and still in 2009. I am a caseworker for the State's Child Protective Services agency long known as the Division of Youth and Family Services, or DYFS, now called the Department of Child Protection and Permanency, or DCPP. I am driving to my last scheduled client of the day, the Pena family. The Pena case is about to be closed based on earlier visits by my colleague, Daniel Garcia. His supervisor has already completed the pink slip approving the closing, so this should be just a matter of paperwork after this last Required Monthly Visit. I might even get home on time tonight. Providing excellent services to New Jersey's troubled families is my pride and joy; that . . . and pride and joy in my own family.

I turn into the driveway of a fairly well kept home, walk up to the house, and ring the bell. It doesn't work, so I knock. I hear a woman's voice muffled from behind the door.

"Coming."

A late twenties Latino woman answers the door smoking a cigarette. She looks gaunt and disheveled. I am taken aback more by her appearance than by the fact that I expected the children's stepfather to answer the door.

"Are you the mom?" I ask.

"No. I'm the babysitter."

I doubt it, but I flash my official State of New Jersey name badge. "I'm Kristin Morris from the Division of Children Protection and Permanency. I need to speak with the stepfather, Mr. Pena. Can I come in?"

The woman hesitates, then acquiesces. "He's not here now. Yeah, come in."

I enter the Pena house and observe three children staring silently back at me. Bella is a crawling one-year-old, Tony is a four-year-old sitting in a diaper, and Jimi is a seven-year-old bare chested in pajama bottoms. All of the children appear Latino.

Since it is shortly after noon, I address Jimi. "Hi, Jimi, I'm Miss Kristin. How come you aren't in school today?"

Jimi shrugs his shoulders. I immediately notice a history of burn injuries on his torso. I try to hide my grimace. "What time will their stepfather be home?"

The woman is evasive. "Don't know."

I turn my attention to Tony and my eyes widen at a fresh burn scar and a black eye. I get closer to look at Bella sitting on the floor and spot a burn on her leg. Tears come to my eyes. I blink them away and say to the toddler, "Hey, cutie."

I look around and begin to survey the house. My jaw goes slack as I see makeshift wiring and exposed light bulbs at every outlet. I walk into the kitchen and see a hole in the floor that reveals the basement. I kneel over it to look in and whip my head back. "You have a sewage problem," I say. I stand and leave the kitchen, crossing the hallway and heading toward the bathroom.

It is filthy and there is no sink. An exposed bulb dangles to the floor. I turn back into the hallway and see a closet door with a padlock. Inside there is a Nintendo. I look to Tony who stares at me with fear in his eyes. I suddenly realize what the closet is used for. I try to reassure him. "It's OK, Tony." I am appalled, and I know I must call this in.

I approach the woman in the living room and say, "OK, I'll have to meet with the kids' stepfather. I'll have to make another visit."

I exit the home and search my casebook schedule for any other visits in the vicinity. I find one and make an uneventful visit, being careful to document it.

Two hours later, I return unannounced to the Pena home. The stepfather of two of the children, Rodolfo, is home and on the speaker phone with his own father.

The older man refers to the four-year-old. "Just beat his ass."

Rodolfo sees me and responds, "Oh, the DYFS worker's here and she can hear you. But she's cool." He hangs up.

I question Rodolfo about Tony's black eye and get a confused series of ludicrous explanations. "He bumped it on the door . . . he bumped it in the pool while playing . . . he came home with it."

I have heard and seen enough. I dial my supervisor Yolanda on my cell. "Hey, Yolanda . . . Kristin. I'm at the Pena house and it's a disaster. I need to remove the kids." I look at wide-eyed little Bella.

Yolanda replies, "Yeah, I understand. Garcia was going to close the case. What the hell was he thinking?"

"I have no idea, but I can't close it now." I continue to look around. The so-called baby-sitter won't even look in my direction. It becomes clear that the Pena children have been through this routine before. They are no longer distressed, and even visibly excited.

"Yay, McDonalds, yay!" Tony calls out joyfully.

Yolanda continues, "I'm good with it. How long do you think you'll be?"

"Mommy, are you coming with us?" Tony asks.

I tell Yolanda to hold on and I ask Tony, "Who is this lady?"

"My mommy."

"No, I'm not the mom, I'm the babysitter," the woman protests.

I step outside for a moment of privacy and get back on the phone. "Yolanda, yeah, the mother was here alone with the children, and there's a court order forbidding it. She's to be supervised 24/7 due to chronic heroin addiction. The stepfather has full custody."

"OK, bring the kids in. Estimated time of arrival?"

"About an hour, after we stop at McDonalds."

"I'll set up the pediatric appointments. You'll need the rest of the day to process the paperwork. See you then."

I walk back inside and speak to the entire family, "The children are coming with me. Kids, get your clothes on. Where are Bella's clothes?"

The mother points to a basket overflowing with unfolded clothes. The two older children quickly throw on their socks, clothes, and shoes. The mother hands me a onesie. I clothe Bella and continue to hold her. Rodolfo stands helplessly in the background.

Jimi and Tony bid farewell to their mother.

The mother's cigarette hand trembles as she smokes with a vacant look in her eyes. She appears emotionless and remains silent.

Jimi addresses me with enthusiasm, "If we're getting McDonalds, can I have a Happy Meal?"

"Yes, Jimi, you can."

As I leave the house with the children, the stepfather mutters curses. We all walk down the front steps to the driveway. The older children smile while we hold hands walking to the car, and I carry Bella. It takes a few moments to put the children in baby and child seats in the state car marked, "For Government Purposes Only." We drive away.

This is exactly what I have come to expect as a case manager in a child protective service agency. I see the worst of the worst and can always be surprised in the saddest fashion. I can only do my job to the best of my ability to meet the needs of these children.

Chapter 2

That evening at DCPP, I complete the paperwork on the Pena children in my cubicle amidst the sound of shuffling papers, ringing phones and distant voices. I am way past due at home. The family will have eaten and readied for bed by the time I am finished.

A fellow colleague, a Hispanic caseworker named Cindy Martinez, comes to my cubicle. "You need to watch your back. You can't be removing kids like this on your own. OK?" The colleague quickly leaves and I shrug my shoulders, wondering what that was about, not taking it seriously.

I'm buried in concentration and totally taken by surprise when Hilda Torres, the Head of Litigation, appears suddenly and aggressively confronts me. "Morris, who the hell do you think you are removing the Pena kids from their home? Who gave you the authority to remove those kids?"

"I'm the caseworker," I protest. "I was assigned to their case. They were in dang–"

"You just dug a hole for yourself so deep you'll never climb out of it," the litigator hisses and storms off.

Confused about these confrontations, I'm disrupted from my paperwork. It takes me a while to get back on track, further delaying my return home.

On the drive home, I begin to wonder if a Latino influence is affecting the way case decisions are being made about abused children. There has been a steady shift in the attitude of management and in the manner in which cases are being handled. It is clearly at odds with the recently established rules and protocols for the newly-acclaimed, data-driven approach to serving the children and families of New Jersey.

At home, I unlock the back door and pass through the darkened kitchen into the dimly lit living room to a muted TV where my husband Benny sits alone.

"You're late," he says.

I'm tired and cranky and snap back, "Don't start with me. I've had nothing but trouble all day . . . a family removal . . . the kids shouldn't have been there in the first place."

"You're the only one doing your job . . . at what price? Sixty hours a week? What about our kids?!"

"I know I work too much, but you're here for the kids."

"I want to raise a family together, not alone . . . it's what you want, too, but your damn job keeps getting in the way!"

"OK! I get it. It's what I went to school for . . . I keep telling you . . . I'll try to move up." There is a pause as we both try to calm down.

"How are the kids?" I ask.

"Gian and Cianna are asleep. Brian just finished his homework."

"Let me go say good night to him."

I go upstairs. Benny follows and goes to bed. Brian seems preoccupied, so I say goodnight and go to bed. I'm exhausted and quickly fall asleep; it is fitful and disturbed. Night turns into day in a flash. Soon it is morning, and I wake the kids. They wander the house in various stages of pajama dress.

Morning sunlight pours into the kitchen as news, weather, and breakfast sounds fill the room. Benny and our three children, eight-year-old Gian, ten-year-old Cianna, and twelve-year-old Brian eat breakfast. Our children look like Benny, with olive skin, brown hair and eyes.

"OK, everybody. Keep an eye on the clock," I tell the kids.

"Mom, she's looking at me!" Gian whines.

"No, I'm not! Stop making stuff up!" Cianna defends herself.

Gian sticks his tongue out at Cianna. She sticks her tongue out back at him.

I look up at the clock. "It's eight fifteen, let's go, let's go. Get your book bags together."

"Have a great day, hon," Benny says and gives me a quick peck on the lips.

"You, too. Remember Brian starts his fall season tonight. What's your schedule like?"

"Home around five. I wouldn't miss it for the world. How about you?"

"I'm in the office today . . . no field work."

"Yeah, but what about emergencies?" he asks.

"We don't have enough state cars to go around."

"For once . . . their screw up works for us."

Benny hugs each of the children in sequence from the back of their chair, placing his cheek next to theirs.

"Bye, Dad," they each respond.

I see Brian stoke his food in. "I hope you're getting enough to eat . . . Your bus will be here any second. Don't forget to brush your teeth," I tell him and ruffle his dark hair.

Brian nods assent with a full mouth, chewing his food.

The school bus engine idles outside followed by a honk. Brian jumps up, kisses me goodbye, grabs his backpack, and hustles out the door without brushing his teeth.

"Cianna, Gian, go brush your teeth, come on, no more playing around," I say.

"Brian didn't brush his teeth," Cianna whines.

"Yeah, Brian didn't brush his teeth," Gian childishly mimics his sister.

"But you will. Your bus isn't here and I have you under my power." I gesture like a sorceress. The kids squeal, jump up and run to the bathroom to brush their teeth.

Benny hurries out and slams his truck door. He gives two goodbye honks and drives away. A moment later a school bus engine rumbles. Gian and Cianna return quickly to the kitchen and hurriedly put on their backpacks. They kiss me goodbye on their way out the door.

"Ugh . . . a toothpaste kiss. I love you," I kid with them.

"Love you, Mom," Cianna and Gian shout, almost in unison.

This day starts out like most days. I have been doing this for six years and I have the home and job routines down. Soon, I hope to seek an advanced degree and move up into the supervisory ranks at work.

I grab my lunch and shoulder bag and hustle out the door.

Chapter 3

I park in the designated lot and quickly walk into a five-story brick building with two cups of coffee. The elevator is empty and moves quickly to my floor. I walk through the door that reads, "The State of New Jersey, Division of Child Protection and Permanency." The scene inside is clamorous.

I walk through a high-ceilinged, fluorescent lit room with over a hundred other workers in cubicles amidst ambient sounds of conversations, keyboards, and phones.

All of my office belongings are in boxes stacked against the cubicle walls. Our office has been moved so many times recently that I have tired of packing and unpacking my entire work area and records. The inefficiency is a plague. Olivia, my colleague and confidant, walks in. She is a thirtyish-year-old Latina woman with a slight accent.

"Kristin, good morning." Olivia smiles broadly.

"Hey, lady."

Olivia sits on the edge of my desk as I key into the computer to access the New Jersey Spirit DCPP dedicated state data storage program.

"Still in boxes, huh?" Olivia asks.

"Why unpack when we'll be repacking any day now? Just working efficiently. Who knows? We could be moving out again by day's end."

"I know. It's such a stylish look. Extra insulation, too," Olivia quips.

"Shush, drink your coffee." I slide one of the cups over to Olivia.

"You're a doll," Olivia says and smiles.

I review the case from the day before in the computerized case management program and share it with Olivia as she sips her coffee. "I saw this family yesterday . . . a real sad thing. Garcia wanted to close this case when there are fifty-four abuse and neglect reports. The mother was court ordered out of the house because of heroin addiction."

Olivia is incredulous. "What was he thinking? So much for the new data driven approach . . . I'll bet they're Latino."

"They are. I had to remove the children. It was tragic . . . Some people around here aren't so happy about it."

Olivia whispers, "Just between us, I've been told in Spanish that we don't put our own out of the house. We do whatever we need to do to keep them in the home."

"But at what cost to the children?"

"The changes were supposed to make things better," Olivia laments.

"The Feds threw money at us, millions, millions . . . the Federal Monitor is a bean counter and the governor is out of touch," I say.

"The governor only sees re-election," Olivia says.

"And not much else," I pause. "But it's the basic issue . . . some people can't change . . . and some people will never be good parents."

"What's the deal with the Federal Monitor?" Olivia asks.

I shake my head. "They have all of these collected statistics show-ing improvements made over the years. But the numbers don't touch the essence of case management . . . and they don't even approach personal agendas that impact case management."

"Yeah, but the agency will never admit to that."

"No, not when politics, power, and money are involved . . . OK, gotta get some stuff done. See you later."

"Later."

I complete paperwork and plan my monthly required visits for the next day. A few hours pass. I visit the ladies' room before lunch. Upon entering I see several colleagues, all Latina. The room goes silent and I feel a shift in the mood.

In the lunchroom, no one looks up at me. I am shunned.

I feel increasingly demoralized and emotionally drained. Criticisms of my work are now the norm. I am constantly questioned and second guessed about my judgment. I speak to the office manager, Hilda Vega Rodriguez, and get only denial and lip service. Hilda acts disbelieving that I could even feel this way and denies everything, but then reassures me that I should continue to communicate my concerns. The leadership staff are predominantly Latino, which has never been a problem before. It was a non-issue. I had heard several workers, Latinos among them, referring to the recent tenure of Hilda Vega Rodriguez as "The Puerto Rican Mafia." I didn't believe it at the time and had paid it no mind.

I have always been a family person, compelled to take care of others, often putting their needs ahead of my own. So, it was no surprise that I elected to major in Psychology in college, or that I thought of service occupations and applied to the Division of Youth and Family Service as a career option. As a new college graduate and a new mom, I was filled with enthusiasm and high hopes of making an impact in the world. I put my heart and soul into my work at DYFS, even to the extent that it sometimes interfered with my own family life. Now that I was being shunned at work, it hurt because I was only doing my job the way I was taught to do it, with the passion to do it well.

At home, I share my concerns with Benny. "I can't believe what's happening at work. I'm being ignored because I did my job with a Latino family."

"You mean the one where you had to remove the three kids?" Benny asks.

"Yeah, it seems that there's some kind of expectation that we're not to remove Latino kids, no matter how bad the situation."

"Why would that make a difference? It shouldn't."

"I know. Olivia sees it too. They even told her that 'we never take our own out of the home . . . we do whatever we need to do to keep them there.'"

Benny tries to be supportive. "Look, you call them as you see them. And you have rules to follow. And you're out there busting your ass to do the best job you can do. What more could they want?"

"It seems that's not the way it works. There's politics involved. And people in power calling the shots. There's a Latino core group that sticks together. I guess you could say they have a power base."

"What will you do?"

"I'll do what I'm doing now—the right thing." I sigh.

"It will work out in the end," Benny says.

Very few people know how hard this job is. In fact, most people don't even think about this type of work at all. When done at its best, it is largely invisible to the public. Only the people directly involved have strong feelings about it, and most of them have very unhappy feelings about child protective services. When we do our job, and take kids away from dangerous parents, we are hated. When we don't do our job, and a child is hurt or killed, we are denigrated and mocked by the general public.

Chapter 4

I have been Jamarr Cruz's caseworker for over a year. I have gotten close to him and have a special fondness for him. Jamarr has been living with his maternal grandparents for a year, ever since he was severely beaten by his mother's boyfriend, Vince Williams. Williams spent forty-five days in jail for the physical abuse, which is rare in New Jersey, highlighting the seriousness of the beatings. Jamarr has flourished in both personal happiness and in school performance while living with his grandparents, Maria and Julio.

Jamarr has had his share of behavioral difficulties. His birthfather was in prison most of Jamarr's life for aggravated sexual assault and was not a presence in his life. Jamarr's mother Omayra and her boyfriend Vince voluntarily completed all of the services offered through DCPP and now they are in a position to push for Jamarr's return to their home. However, completing a program doesn't mean that long-standing behavioral patterns have changed, particularly those that are elicited under stress, or triggered by past vulnerabilities.

Omayra and Vince now have their own baby and there is nothing legally blocking their request for Jamarr. In fact, Omayra could take Jamarr back at any time, since he had never been officially removed from her custody. It is now a matter of completing the Required Monthly Visit, probably the last. Then, I will be off of the case. That is how it is supposed to work in New Jersey. The mission statement is to reunite children with their parents and families. The foster system in the state is a debacle. Yes, there are excellent families. A few even get special training and vetting as "Teaching Families." However, there are the average and mediocre ones, and there are the neglectful and abusive ones who are in it only for the money. Some of these have been in the New Jersey news. Just because a child is removed from an abusive home, doesn't mean they will be placed in an optimum one. The goal of reuniting families is a good one, when it is viable and in the best interests of the child.

I plan my itinerary for the day on the computer and pack my shoulder bag. Olivia walks into my cubicle. I say, "Good morning! Are you ready to go to Jamarr's today? He's the highlight of my day." Jamarr is still with his grandparents and my Spanish isn't very good, so I am bringing Olivia to help me communicate with them.

"Yeah, I'm riding with you," Olivia says.

"Jamarr's about to go back permanently to his mom and her boyfriend. He's had some unofficial home visits. Let's see his file."

"How can he have home visits if the grandparents have custody?"

"Oh, when Vince Williams was incarcerated, the risk was considered to have been removed, so the mother retained legal custody. She could have taken him back at any time."

"So there was no Dodd removal?" Olivia asks.

"No, but Williams is now back in the house." Then I read from the file, "'Vince Williams was sentenced for beating Jamarr with a belt, leaving welts and bruises on his back and hands. He was charged with excessive corporeal punishment and got forty-five days plus probation.'"

"Yeah, I remember now. The pictures were awful," Olivia recalls.

"Williams jumped through all the hoops for six months. He got anger management classes, therapy, and parenting classes. I call him sick but slick. Then he and the mother had a kid together. The baby's about two months old."

"What's going on with this girl?" Olivia asks.

"A lot. Jamarr reported domestic violence. Vince was pushing and shoving his mother. So I visited them back in May. They denied it. They want Jamarr back and the grandparents are willing."

"Let me grab my stuff and we can go."

We leave the office and drive into a poor urban area. Traffic slows. People walk the street and gather on corners. I turn onto a smaller, narrow street, and slow down. Bystanders recognize the marked state vehicle.

"The neighbors know we're here," I say.

Olivia nods. People in their homes spy the government car and quickly shut their doors and pull their shades. I park and we walk up to a brick row home.

"Here it is." I knock on the door.

Jamarr answers with a big toothy smile, "Miss Kristin, you're here. Hi!" He steps outside and gives me a big hug.

"Hi, Jamarr!"

Jamarr speaks to Olivia while his grandparents, Julio and Maria Cruz stand inside the open door. I greet them with my minimal Spanish, "Hola! Buenos días, Señor y Señora Cruz."

Maria is pleasant, but guarded, "Gracias, buenos días señoras, por favor, entra."

Julio Cruz nods. We walk into the family parlor, a small, clean, simple and plain setting with sofa, chairs, an old console floor TV, and a coffee table. Olivia sits and converses in Spanish with the grandparents. I walk over to where Jamarr is sitting on the sofa.

"How are you?" I ask him and smile.

"Fine." Jamarr is beaming. "Come play a game with me!" He pulls me to a shelf where the games are stored.

We sit on the floor to select a board game, but opt for "Old Maid." Jamarr's laughing is infectious and soon we are both giggling.

"How's everything at school?" I ask him after the game.

"OK. My grades are better. I don't get into trouble anymore," Jamarr answers.

"That's great. How's your therapy going?"

"Really good. I talk about things, get them off my mind. He's really nice," Jamarr says, pleased.

"Super! We've been working together a long time now and I need to check with you. How do you feel about going back home for good?"

Jamarr's face transforms from smiles to fear. He begins to tremble. "Is Vince going to be there?"

"Yes." I can see there is a huge problem.

Jamarr stands and pulls me by the hand into the tiny kitchen. His face fills with fear, his eyes well up, and he is shaking.

"I'm afraid of him. I'm scared. He's been mean to my mom . . . he pushed her around. And he hit me again. He makes me do pushups all through the night until it hurts, when everyone is asleep. Don't make me go back," Jamarr pleads.

"Are you sure?"

"Yes, I'm afraid of him. I want to stay with my grandmother. Please, Miss Kristin."

"OK, I got it. I believe you. I'll do everything to keep you here."

Jamarr is terrified. "Please don't tell them. They'll get really mad at me. I'm scared."

"Don't worry. I promise I'll take care of it. I'll start on it right away," I reassure him.

I leave the kitchen and walk into the parlor with Jamarr trailing me and beckon to Olivia. I say, "Buenos días, señor . . . señora," to Jamarr's grandparents, then quietly and firmly, I say, "Olivia, we need to go now."

Olivia speaks to the Cruz grandparents, "OK, adiós, Señor y Señora Cruz."

"Bye, Jamarr. I'll take care of you. I promise," I say on our way out the door.

"Bye. Please don't take too long." Jamarr is petrified.

Once outside, I say to Olivia, "I can't send him home. We can't close the case. He's been hit on visits. He's scared to death. I've never seen him like this."

"You know we're going to have a problem with this. He's not designated high-risk and they hate keeping Latino kids out of the home," Olivia warns.

"I know, I know, but Jamarr depends on me. His safety is my priority." I call Yolanda to brief her on the visit.

"Yolanda . . . Kristin. I just met with Jamarr and conferred with Olivia. Jamarr's extremely afraid of Vince Williams. He is reporting abuse on the visits. He was shaking and on the verge of tears. I believe him." Yolanda agrees to prepare the paperwork before we hang up.

There is a desperate quiet for the rest of the drive.

Chapter 5

That afternoon at the office, I take the lead in starting the process for Jamarr. "OK, let's redo the background checks on the grandparents. You know the drill for a Dodd removal."

"Consider it done." Olivia leaves my cubicle and I walk over to Yolanda's desk.

"We really need to do this. I saw the fear in Jamarr's eyes," I tell Yolanda.

"I agree with you. You know the child best. Process the paperwork. I'll have to get the OK from Aponte," Yolanda says.

She leaves the cubicle with Jamarr's file and walks to the local office manager Mildred Aponte's private office.

"Mildred, hi. How's it going?"

"OK. What's up?" Aponte says in a Spanish accent.

"We need a Dodd to keep Jamarr Cruz with his grandparents. Kristin said he's been hit on home visits. Olivia concurs."

Yolanda hands Aponte the file. Aponte quickly peruses it. She frowns. "I'm not sure you have enough. The family voluntarily completed all of the recommended services." She looks up at Yolanda expectantly. Mildred is not the strongest leader, yet she is one of the barriers to helping Jamarr.

"Yes, we do. The little boy is reporting abuse . . . he's terrified and the history is there. Kristin is convinced and so am I."

"I'll have to run this by Hilda. Let me get back to you in a few minutes."

"OK, but it's getting late and the child is due to be returned to his mother and her boyfriend." Yolanda knows this will be an uphill battle.

Yolanda leaves Aponte to return to Kristin and Olivia. Aponte closes her door and calls Hilda Vega Rodriguez, the fiftyish-year-old Regional Manager, a Hispanic woman with an imposing manner. Mildred is clearly intimidated. "Hilda, it's Mildred, southern office. We're being asked to OK a Dodd for Jamarr Cruz. The kid says he's afraid of the mother's boyfriend."

Hilda is cold and measured. "OK, let me check the records." She enters New Jersey Spirit, the computer client base program, and reviews the summaries. "Hmm . . . No . . . considering what you're telling me, we don't have enough. This is designated a low-risk case. They did everything they were asked to do, so we have nothing to base it on. We're not going to court to get reamed out by the judge and embarrass ourselves like that. So the kid's a little nervous. That's natural. I won't endorse it. Absolutely not. Tell Morris to focus on her high-risk cases."

"OK." Mildred hangs up and comes to my cubicle to tell us the decision. "No, we can't do it. Hilda refuses to endorse it."

Olivia's face is disconcerted. She begins to speak, but stops short before uttering a sound.

But I erupt. "No way. I don't believe it. I'm on the front line. I know Jamarr. This is wrong. We have to slow this down . . . buy time. We cannot send him home tonight."

"There's nothing I can do. Look, I need her 'OK.' Sorry," Mildred walks back to her office looking defeated.

"I'm the one who's been following Jamarr. Why would I press for this if I didn't think it necessary?" I vent to Olivia.

"Yes . . . Yes, I know. I know. We have to make a plan . . . but I'm not sure what." Olivia is angry, too.

"OK. I'll call the mother." I dial Omayra.

"Omayra, it's Kristin Morris," I say, shifting into official mode.

"Hi, Kristin, we're almost ready to leave."

"We have some new concerns and need more time before Jamarr's return. Don't come to pick him up. We'll call you when we're ready."

Omayra's tone changes from pleasant to angry and can be heard loudly through the phone. "What? I'm sick of this, you bitch. I've had it. I want my boy back." She hangs up.

The phone rings and I answer. At that moment, Yolanda walks into the cubicle and hears Vince through the phone. "Damn you, white bitch. You're keeping this kid from us. Who the fuck do you think you are?" Yolanda looks angered that Vince is speaking to her workers with such disrespect.

"I'm done. We'll do what we need to do," I say and hang up. "So much for our anger management program."

Yolanda's cell phone rings. "Yolanda Robinson."

We can all hear Vince through the phone. "Look it, you bitches—" He puts me on edge, like he does every time I visit his and Omayra's new baby. The last time I was there for a required visit, Vince seemed to be hiding something. I heard someone upstairs, but when I asked if Omayra was home and if I could speak with her, Vince said no one was there with us. I began to feel unsafe and left immediately.

Yolanda gets real with Vince and gestures with her free right hand. "No, you look it, big swagga, gettin' all jammed up in my grill. You big man poser all puffed up." Kristin and Olivia glance at each other and look on with astonished amusement. "Why am I even talking to you, fake ass gangsta? He isn't even your son. Put Omayra back on the phone."

Vince complies and Omayra comes back on. "I'm sick of this. We did everything we were asked."

"We're keeping Jamarr with your parents until we investigate,"

Yolanda says firmly. Omayra hangs up on her. Yolanda clicks her phone off. "I'm not sure what they're going to do. Let me know if you hear anything," she says to us and returns to her office.

The windows are dark against the room's fluorescent lighting. It's 8:00 p.m. Olivia and I wrack our brains on how to proceed. Now that Jamarr's mother and her boyfriend know about his report, he could be in real danger; if not tonight, soon. My eyes glaze over as I scan through Jamarr's file on the computer.

"Olivia, I got it. I'll call the Intake Hot Line to send a worker out immediately as an emergency. That forces a stop," I say.

"Great idea. Do it."

I dial the number. "Intake Hot Line, Child Protective Services, Elaine Tory speaking."

"This is Kristin Morris, caseworker for DCPP and Jamarr Cruz. Jamarr needs to be removed from his home immediately. I need an intake worker out there immediately. He expressed fear of his mother's paramour."

"All right," Elaine pauses. "Why aren't you removing the child yourself?"

"My office manager won't approve it. His mother is on the way to get him at his grandparents' home. His mom and boyfriend know about his negative report to me, so he's in danger. His grandmother will give him back without direction from us. We need someone out there immediately."

"I'll see what I can do. We're busy with a lot of calls, but I'll try to arrange a visit. Goodbye."

I hang up and look desperately to Olivia. "I'm not sure if it will be good enough. There is nothing to do but wait." This is not how it's supposed to happen.

"There's nothing else we can do. Let's go home," Olivia says.

"Yeah. Get some rest. See ya tomorrow."

Chapter 6

As the next day at DCPP unfolds, I become increasingly agitated about the absence of any information about Jamarr. As his caseworker, I should have been contacted by Christina Feliciano, the worker sent out to investigate Jamarr's reports. DCPP policy mandates that I be spoken to about my findings and recommendations for Jamarr. I again look at the computer and discover that an immediate visit to Jamarr and his grandparents was not scheduled. I am outraged and stalk to Olivia's cubicle.

"Olivia, they didn't get the worker out like I insisted."

"Since you're already pissed off, I just found out that Omayra and Vince are in the building. They are having the meeting here. Christina is doing the interview here in our offices."

"That's a policy violation. It should be at the child's home. I don't get this at all. What's going on?" I'm in disbelief.

We walk into the hallway as Christina Feliciano, a Hispanic Family Services Specialist II, holds a conference room door for Omayra Cruz and Vince Williams. Vince glares at us. Feliciano avoids eye contact and enters the room. The door closes.

Olivia and I look at each other in bewilderment.

I hear nothing for the rest of that day or the next, or in the days after. The days blend into a week, then two weeks. Neither I nor

Olivia have heard anything about Christina's findings, but we must continue to work our hectic schedules. We have many other children and families to help, but I can't get Jamarr out of my thoughts. I have to find something out.

"I've been trying to contact Christina. Official protocol was for her to speak directly with me and have me complete the paperwork," I tell Olivia.

"It's weird. I haven't seen her around either. Have you looked it up in the computer yet?"

"Many times, but not today. Let's look again." I find Jamarr's file, read and scroll. Olivia looks over my shoulder.

"Son of a bitch. She concluded that there had been no abuse, that Jamarr was safe, and no safety plan was needed. The question was not answered accurately. 'Is the child afraid of his caretaker?' was answered 'No.' Damn it, either she or someone else falsified the document. That was the whole reason I started this. I can't believe this. She concludes that no services are needed. Jamarr will not be removed from his mother's home," I almost start to cry.

"This is not lining up. Something is going on behind our backs." Olivia is flabbergasted.

I walk into the hallway and find Yolanda. She is clearly uncomfortable.

"We didn't want to close the Cruz case! I'm not in agreement with this!" I say to Yolanda.

"I know you aren't, but we have to close the case. Do the paperwork immediately, as soon as you can get to it." Yolanda says, slightly defensive.

"I'm not closing the case. I'm not doing any such paperwork. I want to visit Jamarr again! I need to see him! I know Jamarr's allegation is real! I need to go to see him!"

"No. Let me take the heat on this." Yolanda starts to walk away.

"Are you sure that's the decision you want to make? What happened that I don't know about? I don't understand what's going on here. I'm not closing it and I want to see Jamarr."

"No, you cannot go out to see Jamarr. Close the case. You have too many high-risk cases that need attention and this case needs to be closed."

I return to my desk. I steam and pace about the cubicle. I can't take being inside anymore and leave the building. I go for a walk and while I am gone, Yolanda drops Jamarr's paperwork on my desk. When I come back and find the documents, I glance at them, then walk over to Olivia's desk and hold them up in the air. Olivia is dumbstruck.

"I'm not signing this. They didn't listen to me . . . they didn't listen to Jamarr. This is wrong. I won't sign to close this case."

I leave so quickly that Olivia doesn't have time to respond.

"I'm not signing that." I drop the documents on Yolanda's desk and walk out.

This is the beginning of months of worry. I will not know how Jamarr is doing and I can't see him. I must continue to work as if nothing has happened, when the loss of trust is overwhelming. My mind races. All I wanted to do was to keep Jamarr safe, like I promised. It was just good, basic, by-the-book casework. Now the life of Jamarr Cruz is officially out of my hands.

Chapter 7

My son Brian is playing ball in his fall season. Benny and I support his athletic efforts, particularly in baseball. We try to attend all of his games. Brian is one of the team's stars, both an excellent pitcher and a power hitter. Benny, Cianna, and Gian are there, and I am arriving late from work again.

The infielders chatter to the pitcher as coaches yell instructions in the early evening ball-field. People in the stands talk and cheer. Benny and the children shout from the stands. Brian is pitching and striking out most of the hitters. The umpire gestures again, "Strike three!" Brian retires to the side.

A parent addresses Benny as I walk up the bleachers, "Another one bites the dust. He's got quite the fastball. It's fun to watch."

"We love to watch him play," I say.

"Yeah, he's great," Benny says. He raises his eyebrows at me and smiles to acknowledge my tardiness.

Brian leads off in the home team's final turn at bat. He takes several pitches off the plate for balls. The pitcher hurls again. The bat *pings* as the ball ascends into deep left-center field toward the fence. It clears the fence for a walk-off home run. We all stand and cheer.

The crowd cheers and Brian's teammates chant his name as he circles the bases. Gian and Cianna shout Brian's name among the cheers as they jump and clap. Teammates swarm Brian as he jumps on home plate and walks to the dugout high-fiving his teammates. The stands begin to empty. The coach assembles the players in front of the dugout.

"Great game guys! Way to hang in there! See you all back here tomorrow at five."

The kids collectively respond, "Thanks coach. Thanks. Yeah, right on." Then they offer all-around goodbyes. "See you tomorrow."

Brian finally leaves his teammates to hug us, grinning ear to ear.

"Great game, Brian. That's my boy. Way to go," says Benny.

"Thanks . . . thanks," Brian says, almost giddy.

"Great game! Let's go and have dinner with Grandpa and Grandma. You can tell them about your game-winning home run," I say.

Brian nods and smiles. Gian and Cianna beam at their older brother. The family gets into the car and we head home.

My parents arrive shortly after we get home. They hug the kids and are elated to be with us. There is laughter and joking around the table as we eat and drink. Everyone appears content and happy. I begin the cleanup. My father joins to help me. We place dishes into the dishwasher while the others linger to talk in the dining room. The children play and yell.

"Great meal. Thanks for having us over. It's great to see you two and the kids," my father says.

"Thanks, Dad. The kids love seeing you . . . and showing off for you."

"I'm proud of you."

"I'm proud of us, too, to get our own home. It's what I always dreamed of. Benny and I worked so hard and saved. We've fixed it up just the way we want it."

"You deserve it. Hard work pays off. You can accomplish almost anything if you work for it. How's work going?"

"Great. I love my job. I can really make a difference for these kids and their families. It's hard sometimes, you know . . . the hours are long. I'm not meeting them under the happiest circumstances. I think that I can move up. I know I do good work and I've gotten great feedback. They think my documentation is excellent."

"You always were conscientious. What does it take to be promoted?"

"I should get my masters in psychology, if we can swing it financially. Then, there's placing well on the civil service exam, followed by interviews. I know I'm at least as good as others they've promoted before."

"That's great. If we can help with watching the kids, count us in. Any way we can help with that or household stuff, just ask."

Benny walks into the kitchen. "I think it's time for dessert. I'm sure the kids will agree!" he says.

I bring out pie and ice cream and the kids run to the table laughing. For the most part, all is well, a reprieve from the treadmill of the work week. I try to live my life like it is business as usual. It isn't.

Chapter 8

Several months have passed. I am overworked and constantly tired. My carpal tunnel became too painful and I had to get tendon release surgery. I have been recovering at home. The TV drones as Benny and I sit quietly in our softly lit family room. My right wrist is still bandaged.

"Benny, I need to talk to you about something," I say.

"Yeah, sure. What's up?"

"I know it was months ago . . . but I can't forget about Jamarr. I think about him every day. We talk about him at work sometimes. You know, our Brian actually looks like him . . . they have similar features. Jamarr's mouth is very distinct, like Brian's. I find myself wondering how he's doing, if he's happy, if he's safe. I'm anxious just thinking about him."

"Kristin, you have to stop worrying about every child you meet at work. You're great at what you do; you do your best. You have so many kids to worry about. You did all you could. Let it go. Besides, you're out with this carpal tunnel thing. You're not even at work and here you are worrying. You need to relax," he puts his arm around me and kisses my forehead.

"Yeah, I know, but something doesn't feel right. I have a bad feeling. I can't help it."

Benny takes my left hand into his and holds it while looking into my eyes. "Everything is going to be all right. Let's try to relax."

I try, but I am unable to put Jamarr out of my mind.

———————

The alarm blares at 7:00 a.m. in the dark of my room. Almost immediately, the phone rings. It's Yolanda. I sit on the edge of the bed. A call from Yolanda on my home line is not a good sign.

Yolanda begins, "Kristin, I got a call from one of my contacts at Centralized Screening. He got Jamarr . . ."

"Are you kidding me? You're lying . . . you're lying!" I don't want to believe it.

Yolanda's voice breaks, "Jamarr died of internal injuries. Williams beat him to death."

I become hysterical. I hear the kids begin to stir, but everything is a whirl. I am paralyzed in disbelief. I hang up the phone and cry for several minutes. My fears have come true. Then, Gian and Cianna walk into the bedroom in pajamas.

"What's wrong, Mommy?" Cianna looks concerned.

"Why are you crying, Mommy?" Gian asks.

"Do you remember that little boy, Jamarr, who I told you about? He died. He was beaten to death."

The two children hug and comfort me, but I am inconsolable. The hallway light shines behind Brian who stands speechless and forlorn at the doorway. Benny comes into the room and hugs me. "I'm sorry, I'm so sorry. You did everything you could. It was totally out of your control," he says.

In that instant, I know my life has changed forever.

At about 4:00 p.m., I don't know why, but I call Hilda Vega. I tell her my side of events and I ask for grief counseling. I sense an anxiety in her voice, but it doesn't feel like it is about me, or Jamarr. No one ever gets back to me about the grief counseling, or anything else in an official capacity for six months. Complications with my carpal tunnel surgery keep me out of work longer than I had expected. This organizational silence would be the first in a series of incomprehensible events.

Chapter 9

Weeks have passed since the news of Jamarr's death. I have been bracing myself for the return to a hostile work environment at the same time I have been grieving for Jamarr. My wrist has healed and I feel a calling to my work.

Benny is just about ready to leave for work. "It's raining. The kids' bus just left. Everything OK?"

"Yeah, my wrist is still a little sore, but I'm ready. See you tonight."

"Yeah, see you tonight. Look, it'll be all right," he says and kisses me goodbye.

Benny gets into his truck and leaves. I throw in a load of wash and turn on the dishwasher. Then I go check the mail. It's drizzling outside. I flip through the envelopes and stop when I get to an official letter from work. I stuff the rest of the mail under my arm, open the letter, and read it right there in the rain. The letter is from the State informing me that I have been terminated from my job. The words are like a blur on the page, "Neglect of duty . . . failure to perform . . . egregious and serious neglect of your duties." I feel like my head is leaving my shoulders and floating on air. I rush back into the house and call Benny.

I get the voicemail greeting. "Hey. This is Benny, you know the drill. Leave your name and phone number and I'll get back to you."

I hang up without leaving a message and call Olivia, crying so hysterically that I am almost indecipherable. "Olivia, oh my God, I'm losing my job. I'm not going to be able to support my family. They're firing me for Jamarr's death," I manage to tell her between sobs.

Olivia immediately offers to come over.

We hang up and I call Yolanda. "Yolanda, it's Kristin. They're terminating me. They're blaming me for Jamarr's death." Yolanda tells me they are firing her too, and that Christina got suspended. I tell her to come over and that Olivia is also on her way. We hang up.

I pace the room in consummate disbelief. I talk frantically to the empty room, "How could this be? I did everything I could . . . every-thing I was supposed to do. This has got to be a mistake. We'll lose everything if I lose my job."

Fifteen minutes pass like one. The doorbell rings. Olivia enters the rainy day darkened house with a hooded raincoat. She brushes her hood back. She hugs me in silence and we sit at the table.

"It's got to be a mistake. Maybe the letter was for someone else. You know how they are with paperwork. Is this it?" Olivia asks. She picks the papers up from the kitchen table and shakes her head as she studies the letter. "You did everything you could to get Jamarr outta there. They stopped you. I was right there beside you. We worked on it together. I don't believe this. Did anyone else get letters?"

I nod. "They're terminating Yolanda, too." I shake my head in disbelief. "Maybe I could've done more. I have to search my heart. I don't know."

"Like what? What else was there to do? There were no other options, except to disobey orders and risk losing your job by driving to Jamarr's house in your own car. You would've been fired right then and there," Olivia says.

A moment later the doorbell rings. Yolanda opens the door as she places her folded umbrella just inside. She calls out, "It's Yolanda.

Hello? Can I come in?"

"Yes, come in. We're in the kitchen," I call out.

Yolanda enters and hugs me and then Olivia and joins us at the table. Olivia goes to the counter and makes coffee from a drip coffee maker.

"I never saw this coming. I can't figure it out," Yolanda laments. There is silence for a moment.

"This is totally wrong . . . it just can't be. I did everything right," I say.

Yolanda presents her side. "You have to know my hands were tied. Aponte closed the case and demanded I complete the paperwork. I have my grandchildren to support . . . I never thought Jamarr would be murdered."

Olivia tries to comfort all of them. "None of us did. It wasn't you."

Yolanda collects her thoughts. "We'll have to contact the union."

Olivia agrees. "Yes, we'll need the union's help. Someone set us up." She pauses. "We'll also need God's help. Let's pray."

We join hands around the table.

Olivia leads the prayer. "Lord Jesus, you stayed the course through your suffering even unto your death for our sins. Give us the grace to get through this suffering, give us the strength to always do the right thing, and the faith to see this through until it is done. Amen."

We all end in unison. "Amen."

We continue to hold hands around the table for a few moments. Then we talk for hours about work, our kids, our dreams, our futures, but we have no real plan. None of us know the enormity of what lies ahead.

Chapter 10

The DCPP caseworkers' union, the Communication Workers of America, plans a huge rally that coincides with Governor Corzine's bid for re-election. Corzine's organizers approach the union and cut a deal to avoid bad press for his campaign. All of the fired DCPP personnel linked to Jamarr's death will be returned to work if the union agrees to cancel the rally. The union agrees and Yolanda, Christina and I are returned to work. But there is nothing in writing. No one on the union side thinks this through sufficiently, or knows what to expect in the future, or pins down any commitment from the state's bureaucracy. We haven't seen this particular scenario before. We are reactive, rather than proactive.

Initially, I am mandated to go to New Worker Training in Trenton and Newark three to four times per week for the next two months. I find out that Yolanda and Christina only went for two days. The commute, particularly to Newark, is back breaking, almost two hours each way. When I ask the Administrative Assistant about it, I am told, "Do what the union says." I must continue to attend the training. Finally, I fight the punishment and I am permitted to stop.

During this period, favoritism and discrimination become apparent, even blatant. I am bumped from one supervisor to another. I am not spoken to and not given any clear idea of my work responsibilities.

I have no working state cell phone, no state ID, no access to the e-mail system, or even an access card to get into the building. I must sign in and out every day like a visitor. Sporadically, I am given meaningless tasks, including filing for other workers and copying case files. To top it off, I am totally ignored by the local office manager, Mildred Aponte.

A colleague named Ellen Finley pulls me aside into a conference room one day. I don't know her well at all. Ellen is right to the point. "I did your entire audit. Nothing you did was wrong. You did everything right, but you're being blamed for it. You have to get my report." I agree to follow up, but I have no idea how to get the report.

My union president, Paul Alexander, tells me repeatedly, to the point of badgering me over a dozen times during the next several months, that I must take the deal they are offering of a twenty-day suspension without pay.

Alexander tells me, "If you go to court, it will take two years or more. You have kids. You have to do this for your kids."

I tell Alexander what Ellen has shared with me and still he insists I should take the deal.

I become anxious and depressed, even despondent. Some days, I can hardly get out of bed because I am so depressed. I feel as though I was supposed to keep Jamarr safe, but I was unable to do so. I know I did everything I could possibly do, but I feel guilty for not protecting him. I feel horribly betrayed by DCPP, the agency for which I gave my best, my energy, my time . . . my very soul.

I am advised to pursue arbitration and I get two attorneys from the union to pursue it on my behalf, Anne Marie Pinarski and Molly Richardson. They seem eager and aggressive and they believe in me and my position. It will take a lot of work and time, but I believe that it is worth it.

At home one day, Benny does paperwork at our sun-lit kitchen table. "I think I need to talk to someone about everything. Maybe it will relieve some of the stress. How do I pick a psychologist?" I ask him.

"I don't know. I would do what you're doing . . . go through the insurance list."

I look at the provider list and go through the names, dialing each number in turn. None of the recordings sound hopeful. Several say they are not taking new patients at the moment.

I leave a dozen messages. I had no idea finding a therapist would be so difficult. There are plenty of names, but no takers. This is what it's like to try to find a psychologist from an in network provider panel in New Jersey. Unless you have a referral name, which is by no means a guarantee that you will be seen as a patient, you roll the dice and take your chances.

I dial another number.

"Hello, This is Dr. Zielinski's office. Karen speaking. How can I help you?"

"Hi, my name is Kristin Morris. I need to make an appointment. My job is really stressful and I need to talk to someone. Is Dr. Zielinski taking new patients?"

"Absolutely, yes he is. Let me get your phone number and address and your insurance information. Do you have your card in front of you?"

"Yes, I have the State Health Coverage Plan. I'm a DYFS worker," I give her the insurance information. There is a pause as Karen writes everything down and looks at the schedule.

"I can get you in . . . ah . . . 1:00 p.m. this Thursday, October twenty-sixth."

"I'll take it." I am so relieved.

We hang up. "I actually got an appointment for this week," I tell Benny. "No one else was taking new patients . . . but he is. I wonder how good he is."

"I'm sure he will be great," Benny says.

This is what it has come to. My family needs me and I have to hold myself together for them. Maybe therapy will help.

Chapter 11

I sign in at the front desk with Karen and before I have a chance to sit down, Dr. Joseph J. Zielinski comes into the waiting room. He is middle-aged and wears gold wire-rimmed glasses, pressed khaki slacks, a form fitting dress shirt, and matching tie.

Dr. Zielinski greets me enthusiastically, "Hi! Kristin? I'm Dr. Joe Zielinski."

"Hi. I'm Kristin Morris." We shake hands.

"Please come in. My office is to the back and left." He gestures in the direction of his consulting room. We walk into a softly lit room with ample windows.

Dr. Zielinski guides me, "You can have a seat on the sofa. Please make yourself comfortable."

I sit down and Dr. Zielinski sits in a high backed chair with arm rests, positioned about six feet away. Dr. Zielinski sits back with his clipboard and pen in hand. "How can I be of help?"

"Well, I've worked for DYFS for six years. Things are not what they should be. It got really bad when I needed to go out to close this one child's case." I quickly feel that I can tell him anything. "His name was Jamarr. I went out with my colleague, Olivia, because she speaks Spanish and Jamarr's grandparents don't speak much English. Jamarr was placed with his maternal grandparents after being abused by his mother's boyfriend." I start to cry. "They sent Jamarr back to his mother and just like that . . . he was dead. They're blaming me for Jamarr's death. I don't even have the authority to close a case." I cry harder. "I failed Jamarr . . . but I did everything I could. The details were the worst. Jamarr suffered for hours before he died of internal injuries. The boyfriend admitted to beating him twenty times over six months. He sent the mother on errands to get Jamarr alone. They say Jamarr would stay out to play because he was afraid to go home. He was buried at Clayton Cemetery . . . two miles from here. I couldn't get myself to go to the funeral. I see Jamarr's face every night."

"Why did they send Jamarr back?" Dr. Zielinski asks.

"Because he was from a Latino family. I've been told they do everything they can to keep Latino families together."

"What happened next?" Dr. Zielinski asks.

"First, I was officially terminated for a month. Then, they let me back to work to avoid bad press during the Governor Corzine's campaign for re-election. The union had planned huge rallies, but I was allowed back to work if the union agreed to cancel the rallies. Nothing was ever put in writing. I keep hearing a persistent rumor from my colleagues that Jamarr's mother received four million dollars, her parents a few hundred thousand, and Jamarr's birthfather a lesser amount. There are rumblings about it in the community, too. No one knows the source of the money."

"So! There are politics involved." He pauses. "I'm hesitant to ask . . . is there a birthfather around?"

"Yes, but he spent most of Jamarr's life in prison for aggravated sexual assault . . . he got out about a year before Jamarr's death."

Dr. Zielinski shakes his head sympathetically. "This kid got no breaks."

"No, he didn't." I wipe some tears away. "So, then the union president, Paul Alexander offered me a deal. A twenty-day suspension without pay. He told me that it was time to own up to my responsibility. A child died and someone had to pay the price. I told him I wouldn't accept any punishment until a full investigation proved me negligent. He urged me to take the deal. He said that Christina Feliciano took it. And for this I pay dues through the nose. I told him it was inadequate representation. We found out later that Alexander had misappropriated union funds . . . and that he was schtupping our very own director, Christine Moses. The union has been rendered worthless."

"I've never heard anything like this. How can they punish you if you did everything right? How can they punish you if you didn't even have the authority to close a case? Did you document your work?" Dr. Zielinski leans forward in his chair.

"Yes, I documented everything. They admit that I documented well."

"This is incomprehensible. What have your performance reviews been like over the years?" Dr. Zielinski asks.

"Always very good. No disciplinary actions, very few absences and tardies."

"So, why you? What about the people who made the wrong decision?"

"All of the supervisors are Latino. I'm the only one who stood my ground to keep Jamarr's case open . . . and I'm being blamed. I got heat for removing Latino kids from their home some time ago. I was never treated the same after that."

"Your supervisors made the wrong decision. Whatever the reason, they blew it. If parents are unfit, what difference does it make what ethnicity they are?"

"The emphasis is on the nuclear family . . . but it goes too far when it ignores common sense."

"Kristin, this makes no sense whatsoever."

I shake my head. "No one understands it . . . no one."

"I usually don't encourage getting an attorney, but there are two issues here . . . a Workman's Compensation issue and a discrimination issue," Dr. Zielinski says.

"I have some contacts, including my father, who could help me. I guess this is different than the arbitration attorneys?" I can't afford another attorney.

Dr. Zielinski nods. "There's no question you're depressed, and understandably so. Kristin, I don't know how it's going to turn out. These legal things take time. In the meantime, we have to keep you on track and functioning as best as possible. Any questions?"

"No. Not that I can think of right now."

"Then I'll see you next week. You can schedule with Karen." We stand up and leave the consulting office.

Chapter 12

It has been three months. I have continued to be completely marginalized at work without any reasonable explanation. My fellow workers talk amongst themselves about me. They wonder why Christina is working for Hilda without restriction and why I have no responsibilities. I attempt to key into the computer as I chat with Olivia.

"Still no entry," I say and sigh. "Olivia, I have nothing to do . . . no cases, no phone, no internet. They've made me disappear. I'm out of work at work."

"Looks like they don't want to give you any cases until the arbitration is completed. They think they'll win."

"I don't know how long I can take this . . . waiting for the other shoe to drop. Did I tell you I still have no pass card? I have to sign in each day like a visitor."

"Yeah, I thought that was a while ago, a temporary thing. I had no idea that was still happening." Olivia tries to be helpful. "It reminds me of Kafka's *The Trial*. The guy was accused of a crime, but they didn't tell him what he did. He followed all of the legal remedies to no avail and it went on and on. He never did find out what he did."

"Great. Thanks for cheering me up."

"Sorry. It's just what came to mind. He gets executed in the end." She shoves my arm playfully. "I'm just teasing you now. This really sucks."

"Not too many people know that the local union didn't want to support me on this. They wanted me to take the so-called 'deal.' A guy from the national union went out on a limb, risking his job, to push for me to get support. Now I'm being told that I set a precedent for other workers . . . not to give up and take deals when they're innocent."

Olivia is shocked. "I have mixed feelings about you being a pioneer. Don't get me wrong, you're doing the right thing, and it's not easy. But it shouldn't be that way. What kind of union do we have?"

"I know." I shrug. "I'm going out for lunch. I need some fresh air."

"I have too much paperwork to do. Catch you later." Olivia walks out.

I leave the cubicle area and walk down the hall into the stairwell. I start down the first flight preoccupied in thought, discouraged and befuddled. I pass the first landing, begin stepping on the second flight, and slip on a greasy food wrapper.

I tumble down the last five steps, grabbing at the railing. My belongings go flying. I twist and hit my head at the bottom. A moment passes before a female co-worker enters the stairwell.

"Oh my God." She hurries down the stairs to me. "Kristin, are you all right?"

I sit up on the landing, but I am shaken and in pain. "My back. I hurt my back and hit my head."

Two more co-workers join us and call for help. I get up slowly, but walk out on my own. The first responder says, "I'll take her to WorkNet. You call HR."

I am seen quickly at the ER. Nothing appears to be seriously wrong. I am cleared to go home, diagnosed with a sprained back and given written precautions for a possible concussion. Olivia meets me at the occupational medical site, drives me home, and walks me into the condo.

"Kristin . . . I don't know what to say. It's gotta get better . . . it just has to. You just gotta hang in there." Olivia sits and studies me.

"Is there anything I can get you?"

"No, I'll be OK . . . Ah . . . just shut the lights out . . . Thanks. You don't need to stay." I try to smile. Olivia is uncertain and hesitates, then leaves.

I turn the TV on, then off, and sit in silence in the dark and try to compose myself. I wonder how I ended up like this.

Benny comes home early. I am surprised when he walks in. Likewise, he is surprised to see me. I get up to greet Benny slowly.

"Hey, you're home early. What's going on?" Benny looks at me curiously.

"We're done for today . . . and for the rest of the week. There's no work out there. I don't know what I'm going to do."

"You'll find something, you always do."

Benny's not so sure. "It's different now. I can feel it. It's been tightening up for a while. We were working day to day, but now there's nothing. I've called around. I keep hearing the word 'recession.' I haven't told you because I didn't want you to worry . . . but now you have to know. So what are you doing home?"

"I fell and hurt my back and head on the stairs at work." Benny walks quickly up to me and holds me gently by the shoulders.

"Are you all right? I thought something was off . . . sitting in the dark . . . the way you got up."

"I'm shaken up and I have a headache. I'll probably feel worse tomorrow. Now we're both out of work. Who knows for how long?"

A few days pass and I am starting to move somewhat better. I need to go shopping so I push myself to get out to get it done. I limp around amidst moderate food shopping traffic and run into Dave, a fellow caseworker and union member.

Dave is enthusiastic. "Hey, Kristin, how are you?"

"Dave, hi. Do you want the party line, or the truth?"

"Oh, not so good, huh? Are you back to work yet?"

"They fired me right away, then they took me back for political reasons, but without any duties. They offered me a suspension, but I refused. Now I have to wait for arbitration . . . because I wouldn't take their proposed punishment. I had to take a stand."

"That's totally bogus. I can't believe it. Where's the union on this?" Dave snaps.

"They're done for now . . . after the money scandal. I had to push for representation and I finally got it. I have two lawyers who seem sharp and aggressive, but there's no immediate end in sight. And now I fell and hurt myself at work, so I'm out on Workman's Comp . . . or so it seems."

"I'll spread the word. I can't believe this. Oh my god. Those jerks. Who's behind this?"

"I don't know for sure. Whoever it is, they keep dragging it out and out with delay after delay."

"You know, it might be up to you to look out for yourself. Don't trust anyone."

"It's beginning to look that way." I look at my watch. "Dave, I have to get home to get the kids off the bus. Please give me a call."

"You got it. I'll let the others know what's going down. We all know what really happened. Bye."

I make it home just in time for Gian and Cianna's bus. They laugh and run in, dropping their backpacks just inside the door.

"No snacks until these backpacks are picked up and your jackets are hung up." I command.

Brian comes wandering in. He sees that I am preoccupied. He decides to chirp up. "Mom, what's going on? What's happening to you that we don't know about?"

I am taken aback. "It's job stuff . . . nothing for you to be worried about."

Brian is unconvinced, but elects to let the issue go for now.

Chapter 13

I've been to Dr. Zielinski's office several times now. I never call between therapy sessions, regardless of how much I am struggling. I have a strong sense of boundaries. When I come back for the next session, Dr. Zielinski has no idea that things have gone from bad to worse.

"I was fired again. Now I have no insurance coverage . . . I can't even afford the cost of an office visit." I tell Dr. Zielinski.

"Kristin, look . . . as far as we're concerned, I've got your back. I will see you pro bono as long as necessary to get you through this."

"Really? You'll do that?" I am taken aback by his kindness and generosity.

"Absolutely. You have enough to worry about. I will see you through this until the end, no matter what."

"Thank you, thank you, thank you so much. I really need our visits and I want to keep coming." This was in the pre-Obamacare days, and there was no Affordable Care Act.

"You're welcome. You'll need to try to get some kind of catastrophic coverage for yourself and your family in case of emergencies. Do you know how to get it?"

"Yes, I've helped others get it, never thinking that I'd be doing it for myself."

"Do that as soon as possible. In God's name, what's the basis for firing you?" Dr. Zielinski asks.

"It's got to be that I didn't go along with the punishment. Being out after the surgery just gave them the excuse," I say. "Christina took the punishment and now she's being interviewed for a promotion to Casework Supervisor . . . a promotion!"

"Christina?"

"Yeah, she's the one who did the interview at the office where it should not have been held, and she never contacted me for my opinion . . . as protocol requires. Then, I don't know who did it, but the record was falsified to say that Jamarr was not afraid and not in danger."

"So she played ball from the beginning . . . and she gets rewarded. I see how it works," Dr. Zielinski surmises.

The session continues with a review of recent events as we try to make sense of what is happening. At the end of our time, we leave the consulting office. As I walk out, I tell Dr. Zielinski, "I do have an appointment with an attorney in Philadelphia for an EEOC suit . . . a woman named Edith Pearce."

"Good luck with that. See you soon," he says.

A few days later, I drive into Philadelphia's center city traffic. It is not my cup of tea. Unlike southern New Jersey law offices, I have to pay an arm and a leg to park in a parking garage. I enter the building and go up to the fourteenth floor where The Pearce Law Firm has its offices. I enter and introduce myself. I am told to have a seat and only wait a moment.

Edith Pearce enters the waiting area and invites me in. I begin to tell my story once again. Ms. Pearce is so flabbergasted by what she hears that she prepares to call in a paralegal to record my story.

"Kristin, how long can you stay today? You have a great case and I want to get all of it recorded today."

"As long as I can call my husband to cover the kids, I can stay as long as necessary." I am surprised at her concern, but appreciative.

"Great. Let's get to work." She buzzes her intercom. "Ginny, we need you here right away to record for us." A paralegal enters the room and introduces herself.

I spend the next two hours telling my story. At the end, Edith is very hopeful.

"Kristin, you have a great case. If you want us to represent you, we want to do it. We can have the paperwork drawn up immediately, or if you want, you can take time to think about it."

I can tell that Edith is eager to represent me. Maybe I've found someone who will champion my case. "Let's do it," I say, confident I'm making the right choice.

I leave the Pearce firm with a feeling of hope. In addition to Edith Pearce, I will be working with her associate, William J. Ringland, III. Maybe someone will be able to advocate effectively for me. Maybe someone will be able to hold the State of New Jersey accountable. Maybe, just maybe, I will get my career back.

I then consult a Mr. Howard J. Batt for a Workman's Compensation suit. It is tedious to have to get a different attorney for each issue. However, if they are experts in particular areas, that's how it goes. Once again I explain my story to another professional. I am less confident in this situation. Mr. Batt will periodically request treatment notes and reports from Dr. Zielinski.

The reality is that there is no known or reasonably predictable time frame for either of these cases. It could be years before I learn where I stand.

In the meantime, I do what I need to do for my husband and family.

I shop, cook, clean, and do the laundry. My children do well in school, I help them with their homework when I am up to it, and they stay active in sports. I keep contact with a chosen few at work to see how things are going. I learn that little has changed in the Latino influence on case management decisions. Everyone else is just moving on with their lives. I wonder if the people at fault are even worried . . . if they even care about what happened . . . if they are sad or grieving . . . if they feel guilty. I doubt it.

The State of New Jersey will grind on, maybe even progress without my presence. I feel so small, so unimportant. I wonder how other people's opinions of me reduced me to this. I know I deserve better than this. I am more than just a job . . . but my job was so important to me. I have to pull myself together.

Chapter 14

Christmas is approaching and my parents visit our family's home. They bring a meal. There are Christmas decorations. Amidst family commotion and conversation, my mother plays with her two youngest grandchildren. Brian is preoccupied playing a hand held video game in the corner. Everyone tries to be celebratory, but there is a damper on any real sense of happiness. Everyone knows that things are financially strained.

"Dad, thanks for bringing dinner. We really appreciate it. And the kids are having so much fun," I say and force a smile.

"You're welcome. We love seeing the kids." My father comforts me. We walk back into the kitchen where we like to talk in semi-private.

"Kristin, I don't know why this is happening to you. I wish I could do something to stop it. I feel helpless. There must be a reason for it. Maybe we just can't see it yet."

"I don't know, Dad. When I tell people about it, it sounds so bad they look like they don't believe it, like I'm making it up. I know I want something to come of this. Not only do I want my job back . . . I want kids to stop slipping through the cracks."

"That might even make it worth it, if it doesn't destroy you first."

"When I went into this field, I knew I would see victims. I never thought I would become one myself."

He looks down. "Kristin, you're young. You've never seen how things really are. They are not what they seem, and they are not what they should be. Look, there's no way you could have seen this coming. But this kind of stuff happens all the time in New Jersey. We don't know most of it, but now you're seeing it . . . and it's nasty," he says.

"The worst part is I know you're right. My psychologist can't believe it either. He says I should try to make it public."

My dad nods emphatically. "Yes, I agree. What's holding you back?"

"My lawyers, they think I have a good case, that I should play it out and keep the idea of going public as a potential bargaining chip."

"I suppose the professionals are advising you on one course of action. I don't know. I've never been in this kind of squeeze myself. It could go either way."

The afternoon and evening pass slowly. The children quiet and settle down. My parents tire and the two little ones are ready for bed. My parents leave around 10:30 p.m.

Benny kisses me and says goodnight. I change into my gym clothes, grab my keys, put on a jacket, and quietly leave. I start the car, hunt for a good song on the radio, and begin to get energized by the music. I feel more awake now.

I walk into the gym and greet Matt, the desk attendant. The gym is filled with the sound of rock music, the hum of fans, and the clank of weights and other gym equipment from a few night owls working out.

"Hi, Matt! How's it going?"

Matt is his usual over-the-top, enthusiastic character. "Kristin, our nighttime lifetime member. It's going. How are you feelin' tonight?"

"I'm pretty sore, but I have to keep going."

"Yeah, you're right. Have a great workout."

I head to the treadmill, step up, and start plodding. I am tight and uncomfortable from back pain, but I gradually loosen and speed up a little at a time. My face gets red and glistens with sweat. I begin to feel a sense of accomplishment. This is the only thing I have control over. I finish my workout, drive home, shower, and drop into bed.

Morning arrives way too soon. I don't want to get up, but I force myself to get the kids off to school. Benny has been depressed and out of work himself, and his irritability has only gotten worse. My depression is impacting the entire family. We get through the morning routine and see the kids off on the bus before coming back inside. There is a message on the answering machine.

Benny presses the voice mail button. "This is an attempt to collect on an overdue—"

Benny hits delete. "The message has been deleted."

"Hear that? There's no money, not even for the mortgage."

"What are we going to do?" I ask.

Benny erupts. "You should've taken the punishment. You would've been back to work and we wouldn't be in this situation."

"I thought you were with me on this. I did nothing wrong. I'm being scapegoated. I'll never admit to doing something I didn't do. I can't believe you just said that." I am shocked and hurt, near tears.

"I'm sorry, I didn't mean that. I don't know what to say . . . I'm going for a walk." He storms out.

I wonder how much longer the family can go on like this. This is not the way to live, and this is not what I worked so hard for. We may lose our home. The kids feel the stress, and our marriage is in trouble. Was Benny right? Did I make the wrong decision? Maybe I should have played ball. It keeps dragging on and on. Nothing happens for months at a time. I am just a blip on the radar. The State of New Jersey marches on. They are working and getting paid. They can provide for their families. I do the right thing and I am on the cliff of disaster.

Chapter 15

At Dr. Zielinski's office, I feel supported in my therapy sessions. I tell Dr. Zielinski the latest news. "Because of the fall at work, I have headaches and back pain. Between Workman's Comp, IMEs, and Medicaid, you wouldn't believe how poorly I'm being treated. They cut off my Workman's Comp."

"Who did you have to see for the psychological IME?" Dr. Zielinski asks.

"Dr. Holl?"

"Dr. Holl is unprofessional. It's common knowledge around here that he's a hired gun who always works for the insurance side. They send people to him because he's a 'licensed professional' who will say what they want him to say. The Workman's Compensation situation in this state is a disaster, the worst case of the fox guarding the henhouse I've ever seen."

"I also had to see an orthopedic surgeon," I continue. "He was arrogant, disinterested, dismissive, and spent only five minutes with me. I knew I was in trouble from the get go. During the exam, he asked me to perform some exercises, and my range of motion was obviously limited from being in so much pain. He sent me to physical therapy, and after only five visits, he sent me for an orthofunctional assessment at a place in south Jersey . . . ProForm. I went there not knowing what to expect. I spent two hours working with several physical therapists. I was asked to carry boxes and stack them. Then, I had to pick up boxes of different weights and put them down. The staff barely spoke to me and gave me very little feedback. Finally, one of the physical therapists tells me if I can't do anymore because it hurts too much, it's OK to stop. So I stopped. I left with no idea of how I had done."

Dr. Zielinski shakes his head and says, "Workman's Comp likes to keep people in the dark."

"Then, I had to go back to the orthopedist. I actually heard him discuss me on the phone with ProForm through the wall of the adjoining room. He said he needed my results for the evaluation. Then he became arrogant and said, 'Oh, no, no. She didn't put in enough effort. I know you'll do the right thing.' He came back into the room and told me I was being cut off from benefits because I didn't put out full effort. I defended myself and told him I needed an MRI. I told him I heard what he said, what he told ProForm to write in their reports. He told me I would have to fight that out with my lawyer!" I am exasperated all over again from retelling the story.

"Unbelievable," Dr. Zielinski says and scribbles some notes down.

"Yeah, I also found out that the State's Workman's Comp is run by our own dedicated State Insurance Department."

"Yeah, dedicated to who, the CEO?" Dr. Zielinski asks sarcastically.

"Then, I had to go back to the neurologist. He's an older man, looks like he's nearing retirement. He wouldn't evaluate or speak to me further. He simply said, 'I heard about the orthopedic results. They're cutting you off from your benefits. I'm not going to be the last man standing . . . I'm sending you back to work.' I tried to reason with him. 'But you're a neurologist, a different specialty. I'm still getting headaches.' He totally dismissed me. He said, 'There's nothing left to discuss.' And he walked out of the room.'"

Dr. Zielinski is agitated. "I don't know how these doctors can look themselves in the mirror each morning. How much do insurance companies pay them to behave like this?"

"I'm not sure, but it must be substantial." I take a deep breath and continue. "Then I had my first Medicaid experience. I felt bad for myself, but I felt worse for the other people. I had to go to a clinic in Camden because of my Medicaid insurance."

"I'm sure that was a treat." Dr. Zielinski shakes his head.

"It was cloudy and looked like it was about to rain. I drove to the clinic in a Camden ghetto, a new building amidst older buildings. Prostitutes loitered on the street. I entered the facility and I was startled to see a security guard who nodded to me. There were mostly African American people of all ages in five rows, stark white walls, and a line at the receptionist's window. Many of the people stared at me. One of the patients says, 'They're behind already.' Another responds, 'What else is new?' I gave my name to the receptionist and sat down. I waited for three hours. I was irritated beyond belief. I asked the woman next to me if it always took this long. She told me she always gets there early in the morning and hopes to be seen before the clinic closes. Then, a sixty-ish-year-old clinic doctor entered shamelessly late and greeted the female staff. It had been five hours by then. The doctor displayed no urgency. He laughed and joked with every staff person behind the glass. A middle-aged black woman in the row ahead of me quietly turned around and told me, 'This guy is nasty. He'll flirt with you and offer to give you a breast exam. I don't want to scare you, but every time I'm here, he wants to give me a breast exam. He does that with every woman.' I thanked her for the warning."

"What?" Dr. Zielinski is unsettled. "Where do they find these doctors?"

"After twenty more minutes, I was finally called by a staff member and escorted to an examining room where I waited twenty more minutes. The doctor entered, and barely looked me in the eye. He asked me why I was there and I told him because of stress. He listened to my heart and lungs. He asked me who my usual doctor was. I started to tell him that Dr. King sees me for asthma and depression but the doctor interrupted me and said, 'You can only be seen for one medical problem per visit. I don't agree with your medications. There are too many and the dosage is too high.' I tried to tell him that you faxed over documentation on why I need the meds and how I'm doing well on them, that there's a release for the doctors to discuss it. He said he had no release and that your office should fax it again. Then, he asked if I needed a breast exam!"

"I'm disgusted. New Jersey Medicaid is pathetic . . . lower class medicine for poor people. Why do you have to go through this? What about going public with your story? Like I said before. You could explode this thing into hell where it belongs," Dr. Zielinski says.

"Everyone says I should, except my lawyers. They think I have an excellent case and the threat of going public could be leverage. And I don't want people to get the wrong idea, that this is just about me."

"Always do what feels right for you in your heart." He pauses. "Remember. The invisible knot is tighter. Sometimes our greatest strength is also our biggest weakness."

I look at Dr. Zielinski quizzically through another long pause.

Dr. Zielinski continues, "Like when is doing the right thing . . . not the right thing? And if they put a gag order on you, this will never come out."

"Which is not what I want. There are other abused children who need protection. I won't let them sweep this under the rug." I pause for a moment, then say, "I might want to write a book . . . would you help me? I'm a lousy writer."

Dr. Zielinski has to end our session and he avoids answering the question. "Let's see what happens. Our time is almost up. Anything else before we wrap it up?"

"I feel awful for my kids. There's nothing for Christmas. We can barely put food on the table. In the past, we would collect food for other families who needed it."

Dr. Zielinski tries to be hopeful. "Maybe someone will step up to help you the way you helped others. You never know. I'll see you next week."

"OK, see you next week."

I leave the consulting office, scurry to the ladies' room and return for my coat. As I pass by Karen's office, she calls, "Kristin, I have something for you." I walk up to her desk. Karen keeps a straight face. "Santa dropped this by for you." She hands me an envelope, a Christmas card addressed to "Kristin and her family."

"Thank you. Merry Christmas, Karen," I say.

I leave the office and hurry to my car. "Little Drummer Boy" plays at low volume on the radio. I open the envelope and the card. Ten one hundred dollar bills spill into my lap.

I gasp, and start to cry. For joy, for sadness, for good people in this world.

The card is signed, "Merry Christmas! You are the bravest person I know. Santa." My tears drip onto the card.

Our family will have a Christmas.

Chapter 16

New Year's Day comes and goes and we are back in reality. The children are going back to school after their Christmas vacation.

Benny is out looking for work. I struggle through the morning routine. Brian gets himself going. I pour bowls of cereal. Brian slurps milk and runs out the door as his bus arrives. A few minutes later, Gian and Cianna kiss me and get on the bus. "Have a great day. I love you," I tell them.

I walk back into the bedroom and sit on the edge of the bed. The clock radio shows 8:30 a.m. I fall asleep and hours go by.

The loud engine of the school bus idles in front of the house as children squeal. The clock radio shows 3:15 p.m. The kids are home.

Cianna and Gian call for me in unison. "Moooomm! Mooomm!"

I walk out slowly to greet them, rubbing sleep from my eyes.

"Mommy, did you sleep all day?" Cianna asks.

"No, honey, I just laid down for a few minutes. Let's get a snack and we can start your homework."

Gian and Cianna hug me and we sit together on the couch. Brian walks in from school.

"Hi, Mom . . . Hey, Gian . . . Hi, Cianna." He goes to his room.

Cianna says, "Mom, now you're home more but all you do is sleep."

I hug her and manage to say, "I'm sorry, honey."

Some days I am so depressed that I can only do the bare minimum, only what I must absolutely do. I am embarrassed by my incapacity, but I am unable to alter it. One day fades into the next. My life is in shambles through no fault of my own. It is the effect on my family that is the worst to bear.

***

The State's attorneys have been dragging the arbitration out longer and longer by rescheduling again and again. Each cancellation results in a six-month delay. Their attitude toward the issue is cavalier. One cancellation is because of one of my own attorneys. Another occurs halfway through a hearing day when the State's lead attorney, Nicole Colon, has to leave at the spur of the moment.

Ann Marie Pinarski says to me, "Nicole Colon has no child care coverage. She needs to leave at one-thirty."

"Wait a minute. We all made arrangements for child care. This was scheduled months ago. This is unacceptable. Just when is the next hearing going to be scheduled?" I'm incensed.

"Of course we'll have to work that out. I can't tell you right now."

"Look, my life is on hold. Everybody else just goes ahead with their lives. Each delay costs me financially and emotionally," I say.

Ann Marie goes deadpan. "It's not up to just me. I have to go along with the schedule they set up. You could have taken the deal . . . and it would have been over. Why do you want to do this?"

"Because I did nothing wrong! In fact, I did everything right."

Ann Marie gets serious. "Kristin, you need to know that the chances are very high that you're going to get some disciplinary action. At a minimum, you'll get five days of disciplinary action. I have to let you know what you're facing . . . They have to split the baby."

Months later, just before the start of the second hearing date, John, a representative from the Department of Labor, a man whom I have never met, almost convinces me to take the deal. He drives with me to Trenton and rambles some unusual beliefs. "Spare the rod, spoil the child," he says, eyes straight ahead on the road.

He goes on, "I don't even know why we're doing this, we shouldn't even have a DYFS."

I remain silent.

"You're not going to get a fair decision. You should take the deal," he says, matter of factly.

This guy is supposed to be on my side, but he is clearly telling me I have no choice. I almost break, but when we arrive, I hold true to my convictions.

I'm now more sure than ever. I look at John as he parks and announce, "If the arbitration finds me culpable, even some, I'll take whatever punishment they mete out . . . I need to find out what they'll decide after they hear everything."

When I tell Ann Marie, she is slightly taken aback by my resolve.

It is approaching two years of waiting. No one really cares on a personal level what is going on in my life.

I never had a need to know the size of the Attorney General's Office before now. I become aware that the State has an army of attorneys on the payroll, so this delay doesn't cost the State a penny. Conversely, anyone who represents me will have limitations on how much time they can devote to me and on how long they can afford the arbitration hearings to last. The State of New Jersey works like a big machine with a staggering inertia that always works to its benefit. I'm a small irritant matter that they plan to dispose of at some time in the future, when they get around to it. This case is big to me, but it is one among many in their cumbersome system.

Several months more go by. But now the time has come. Rusty, depressed, tired or not, I must steel myself for the upcoming arbitration and its preparations. At least this will help me structure my aimless and empty days. And it will bring me closer to vindication and a return to work.

Chapter 17

I meet with my attorneys, Molly Richardson and Anne Marie Pinarski, to prep for my up-coming arbitration hearings. Pinarski drives the process.

"OK, break time is over. The testimony could go all day long. We have two more hours here. We did the easy stuff. However, on cross, it will be very different. Ready?"

"Yes," I say quietly.

Pinarski assumes a domineering and authoritative tone and stands over me.

"So, Ms. Morris, you state that you did everything you could to save Jamarr Cruz.

Clearly, you didn't do enough. He died. Why didn't you push further?"

"Well, I followed all the procedures—"

"So good casework is about following procedures."

"No, of course not. I tried to do more, but I was told that I couldn't."

"Why would that stop you when a child's life was at stake?"

"I didn't know what else I could do. I—"

"So, a child died because you didn't know what to do. You were his caseworker. He depended on you. What can you tell us about that?"

There is a long pause. "I feel terrible. I think about Jamarr every day."

"Feeling bad doesn't bring the child back. He's dead forever. Could you have done more?"

"I don't know."

"You don't know? Six years in the field and you don't know what to do. You know what to do to start lawsuits. You have a mental health suit . . . an EEOC suit. Is this about you, or is this about Jamarr Cruz?"

I start to cry and Pinarski looks at Richardson with a look that says "I told you so." Pinarski breaks role. "Kristin, you need to take the deal. If you fall apart like this, you'll look guilty even though you're not."

"No, I can do this. Let me try again." I wipe my tears and try to muster up my resolve.

Richardson adds insult to injury. "DYFS is not cooperating with discovery. None of the paperwork documenting your work has come through and they are calling the auditor's report confidential, making it unavailable. Information they didn't admit to evidence during discovery is in the auditor's report. They're not getting back to us, they're delaying all over the place."

Pinarski adds, "I've never seen anything like it. It's like something huge is at stake, something over and above your hearing." She shakes her head, perplexed.

"But we need Finley's report . . . it has the data. It will prove that I did everything I could, and everything I said I did." I am desperate.

Richardson is adamant. "They're saying you didn't make the required monthly visits. That's what we're dealing with. They're stonewalling us. By the way, what's this list of forms?" She hands a list to me. I study the document.

"This is the master list of the documents I used. It's not the documents, but it lists what I did. It's a log. I can testify from this." I start to feel excited.

Pinarski is surprised. "They let it slip through . . . OK, maybe we can do this. Let's run through it again. Remember, they're going to press you on the fact that a child died. You have to answer the facts and not get caught up in your emotions. Face it, they don't really care what you did or didn't do!"

"I can do this." I have regained my confidence.

———

Several months pass and I have been feeling better mentally and physically. However, my mood still varies and there is no rhyme or reason as to how my emotions flow. It is part of the State's strategy to wear out opponents by allowing them to use up their resources, as in the sieges of old . . . a war of attrition.

My gym workouts have gone increasingly well. I enter the gym for a morning workout with headphones draped around my neck. Matt is at the front desk. Rock music plays and gym equipment clangs.

"Hi, Matt. I haven't seen you in ages. How's it going?"

Matt looks up, surprised to see me. "Hey, Kristin! . . . Super! I was promoted to day shift. Wow, aren't you looking great."

"Yeah, I'm feeling pretty good most days." I grin broadly and giggle.

I walk to the treadmill and begin to work out. I put my headphones on to listen to my favorite rock music. I start slowly, but warm up into a full run. I begin to daydream recent happier events. They run through my mind in a stream of consciousness. I smile faintly as I recall happy images.

. . . My family as they all smile and eat breakfast at our home . . . My parents around the dining room table . . . Talking to my father in my kitchen... Laughing with Olivia at work . . . Jamarr's smile . . .

I'm almost done with my workout. I finish with a flourish. I come back to the present. The sun shines on me through a very large window as I step off the treadmill, remove my headphones, and face the window.

Matt looks at me with pride. He shouts on the sound system, "Kristin's in the building now!"

I smile. Today is a better day, if only for now, if only for today.

Chapter 18

Olivia, Yolanda, and I meet for lunch at a local diner. It is crowded and noisy, but we focus on each other and try to enjoy our meals. None of us are happy.

"Well, maybe you heard. I was demoted and given a four-week suspension without pay," Yolanda says.

"Oh my God! Why?" Olivia gasps.

"I'm so sorry. It's not right." I say.

"It's my punishment for following orders . . . I was damned either way," Yolanda says.

"Yeah, promote the people who made the mistakes . . . what is that?" Olivia pulls in closer. "Something is going on. I needed to see you both. It's not pretty. I've been pressured by Hilda Vega and the State attorney to alter my testimony . . . to minimize what you did to save Jamarr."

I look at Olivia stone-faced.

Olivia continues. "I refused, but they threatened me with a five-day suspension for insubordination."

"I can't believe they would stoop to this level . . . but I heard the same from Ellen Finley. She called me. They've pressured her, too," I tell them. "Thank you, Olivia, you're a real friend . . . and a real pro."

"Even pressuring the auditor! They're willing to do anything to win. How do they just get away with this?" She thinks for a moment. "We have to report this."

"My attorneys are pursuing the auditor's reports," I say.

"What the hell is going on here? Moses was promoted to Assistant Commissioner of the Division of Families, in charge of Quality Control. How ridiculous is that?" Yolanda is beginning to get upset.

"Who's pulling the strings on this? It looks like I'm going to have to take care of things myself," I say.

We finish eating in mixed disbelief and anger. We have no clear plan on how to proceed. Yolanda leaves first. Olivia and I follow a moment later and exit the diner.

The State of New Jersey, as represented in the personnel of its official employees, is not interested in justice. They just want to win, at any cost of decency and fair play. Why is this so important to them?

<hr />

My attorneys pursue the admissibility of the Auditor's Reports. Apparently, this is the first time in arbitration history that DYFS has challenged their admissibility, setting a legal precedent. Briefs are written by the attorneys from both sides and the arguments are reviewed by a judge. The judge opines that the general report should be admitted, but that the Auditor's report should be withheld because of its conclusions, which were termed 'opinions.' No one knew exactly what these opinions were, but the fact that the State of New Jersey fought their admissibility would logically lead to the supposition that they found the opinions unfavorable to their position.

Here's the kicker. My arbitration attorneys report the witness tampering effort. It stops, but there is no legal repercussion for the attempts.

I try to force the issue several times with my attorney. "This is a big deal. Why should these women be subjected to this pressure?

Surely this is illegal."

Ann Marie repeatedly and simply responds with, "I took care of it."

Sometime later, well after the arbitration decision was rendered, Dr. Zielinski tries to resurrect the issue in an effort to exact some justice in the matter. He receives a return phone call from Anne Marie. She is curt and to the point, and tells him she put an end to it. She stopped the pressuring. As for the director, she was a terrible witness and Anne Marie took care of her that way.

It appears that there are no censors, write ups, or even corrective verbal interventions for the irregular activities. They are simply told to knock it off. The typical observer would see their efforts as illegal and worthy of legal sanction. I conclude that my attorneys did, and will continue to, work with the State of New Jersey's legal team, and they must maintain some type of rapport.

In short, the State of New Jersey's personnel can take all risks at will, without consequences. They continue to act in self-serving fashion without compunction.

Chapter 19

The arbitration is held in the New Jersey State House in a large conference room. It is 9:00 a.m. Mr. Jeffrey Tener, about sixty, is the designated arbitrator. He is dapper, wearing a suit with a bowtie. Nicole Colon is the State's lead attorney. Christina Moses, mid-forties, is the State Director of DCPP. Moses is slightly nervous.

The court official begins. "Please state your full name for the record."

"Christina Moses."

The official continues. "Please raise your right hand. Do you solemnly swear that you will tell the truth, the whole truth, and nothing but the truth, so help you God?"

"I do."

Colon begins her questioning. "Ms. Moses, what is your job title?"

"State Director of the Department of Child Protection and Permanency."

"What is the scope of your duties?"

"I directly supervise twelve area directors, have responsibility for operations and policy, and handle critical incidents."

"When did you become involved in the Cruz case?"

"When the child Jamarr Cruz was murdered."

"Are you entirely familiar with the Jamarr Cruz case?"

"Yes, I have reviewed all of the relevant documents. I reviewed the child's record and made a report to the Commissioner."

"In your assessment of the case, what did you find about the professional behavior of Kristin Morris, Caseworker on the case?"

"Ms. Morris did not react appropriately on September seventeenth, two-thousand and eight, when the child informed her that he was being hit by his mother's paramour when in his mother's house."

Moses is smug. I fix my stare on her through her entire testimony. Moses looks at me once, then avoids eye contact.

"Ms. Morris did not report the problem to DYFS until the next day and she never saw the child after that. She later had a conference in a hallway with her supervisor to close the case. She agreed to the closing of the case despite seeing the child's fear and the previously documented history of serious physical abuse."

Tener looks concerned and watches Moses.

"Ms. Morris could have told her supervisor that she had not completed the final monthly required visit, that all of the recommended services had not been completed, and that the case should remain open. Ms. Morris failed to think critically and use proper judgment. She grossly neglected her duty as the child's caseworker. She can no longer be trusted to ensure the safety and well-being of children under the care of DYFS." Christina Moses repeats bold faced lies to everyone. "Ms. Morris failed to recognize, document, and respond to red flags that were evident throughout the case."

Tener takes more notes.

"There is no indication from the May thirtieth, two-thousand and eight visit that Ms. Morris responded to the child's report of the paramour's physical abuse of his mother and his expressed fear," Moses continues.

My lawyers Pinarski and Richardson shake their heads with disgust, take notes, and frown. I write the word 'perjury' on a slip of paper and slide it to Pinarski.

"On the visit of September seventeenth, two thousand and eight, when the child expressed verbal and behavioral fear of returning home, Ms. Morris did not take steps to remove the child and left him in total fear. She should have initiated a Dodd removal."

Colon glances at her notes. "Ms. Morris called the Intake Hot Line, but classified the case as within twenty-four hours, rather than as an emergency."

I shake my head in disbelief.

"Ms. Morris did absolutely nothing to protect the child. She should have had a face-to-face meeting with the child to assess his statements."

Colon finishes. "What final conclusion can you draw from your review of the case?"

"As the caseworker, Ms. Morris had extensive information about which she should have alerted management. She should have argued against closing the case, but she chose to do nothing and utterly failed to advocate for the child. Her discharge must be upheld."

"I have no further questions. Ms. Pinarski, your witness."

Pinarski begins her cross examination. "Ms. Moses, were you supervising the Jamarr Cruz case in any capacity before his tragic death?"

"No, I was not."

"Ms. Moses, isn't it true that the first time you reviewed documents on the case was almost six months after the child's death?"

"Yes, but—"

Pinarski interrupts. "So, Ms. Moses, you only became involved long after the events in question?"

"Yes."

"Ms. Moses, is it true that there is pressure on caseworkers and their supervisors to close low-risk cases as quickly as possible to reduce caseloads to fit the agency's operating model?"

"No. DYFS is responsible for the safety of children and no policy would risk the life of a child to provide lighter caseloads."

"Yes or no, Ms. Moses, isn't it true that the Jamarr Cruz case was officially designated as a low-risk case?"

"Yes, but–"

Pinarski interrupts her sharply. "No buts, Ms. Moses. Isn't it true that Ms. Finley's report as the DYFS auditor indicates that Ms. Morris had documented the case very well?"

"Yes."

"Ms. Moses, you have testified that Ms. Morris did not effectively document her professional activities. Why the difference?"

Moses gets increasingly uncomfortable as Pinarski exposes her testimony to be false. "Yes, when she did document, as in her case notes, she documented well."

"Ms. Moses, were all of the documents that you reviewed made available for the Union's review of this case?"

"Yes, of course."

"Ms. Moses, that's puzzling, because neither I nor my assistant counsel received many of the documents that we requested. What do you know about that?"

"Nothing. I'm not aware of that."

"Actually, we will work around that. I have a list of documents that were created by Ms. Morris as she completed her professional duties. Ms. Moses, would you please review this copy of the list that indicates what documents Ms. Morris completed during the course of her work with the child and his family?"

Moses glances at the list for a moment and looks up very concerned.

Pinarski pounces with sureness and a bit of sarcasm. "Ms. Moses, please go ahead, please go through the list for us and tell us what each entry means."

"Well . . . the first indicates that each monthly required visit was completed." Moses pauses. "The second indicates that Ms. Morris implemented multiple services for the child as well as his mother and her paramour." Moses pauses again. "The third indicates that she made several attempts to remove the child from the home after identifying an imminent risk of harm."

"Ms. Moses, is there any evidence that any of Ms. Morris's supervisors told her that she should do more, or do something differently throughout her handling of this case?"

"No, but–"

Pinarski interrupts her. "'No' is sufficient. Ms. Moses, what does the fifth form on that list indicate?"

"That's the form for a Dodd removal of a child . . ."

Pinarski interrupts. "By whom, Ms. Moses?"

"Ms. Morris."

"Ms. Moses, isn't it true that Ms. Robinson, Ms. Morris's supervisor, went to Ms. Aponte, who went to Ms. Rodriguez, to institute the Dodd removal and that it was refused?"

Moses is confused. Her testimony has just been eviscerated. "I don't know." Moses is looking down and a red blush shows on her neck and upper chest.

"Well, Ms. Moses, you stated that you reviewed all of the paperwork. How would you explain this situation to the Federal Monitor, Judith Meltzer?"

"I don't know."

"No further questions."

Tener orders a recess. "We'll stop for now and resume in the afternoon."

Chapter 20

The hearing continues with me on the stand. I have finally gotten my day to be heard.

Pinarski begins her examination. "Ms. Morris you have been sworn in. Are you the caseworker who worked with the Cruz family?"

"Yes," I answer, feeling confident.

"Ms. Morris, what did you do when the child told you of his fear of his mother's paramour?"

"I consulted immediately with my colleague, Olivia Figueroa, and we called Ms. Robinson from the field. Then we returned to the office and immediately began the process for a Dodd removal."

"What happened after that?"

"Ms. Aponte and Ms. Rodriguez refused to allow it. I began arguing my position. I was upset and in disbelief."

"Ms. Morris, what happened next?"

"I called Jamarr's mother and told her to hold off picking her son up at his grandmother's to buy time. The mother and her boyfriend were furious."

"What did you do next?

"I immediately called the Intake Hot Line and pressed for an immediate emergency visit to the child's home to assess his fear and the risk."

"Ms. Morris, why did you do that?"

"First to buy time. Then, to get an independent assessment. My report that the child expressed fear of his caretaker mandates further assessment of the family and blocks his return home."

"How did that work?"

"They ignored my request for immediate assessment and opted for a twenty-four-hour assessment. Then they did the interview at our office, not at the family home . . . which is a policy violation. Then, they did not speak with me, as is required protocol."

"Ms. Morris, what happened after that?"

"There was a delay of two weeks, during which time I should have been consulted by Ms. Feliciano . . . but I was not. Then, I discovered on my own in the computer records that the child's report of being afraid was deemed unfounded, that the record had been falsified, and that the case was to be closed."

The room is hushed. "Ms. Morris, did you agree with that?"

"Absolutely not."

"Did you participate in any way in the closing of the Jamarr Cruz case?"

"No."

"Ms. Morris, did you sign supporting paperwork for the case to be closed?"

"No. I refused."

"Did you ask to see the child again?"

"Yes, several times. I asked Ms. Robinson and I was told no each time."

"No further questions. Your witness, Ms. Colon."

I begin my testimony under the State's cross-examination.

"Ms. Morris, you are still under oath. Earlier you testified that you did everything right. How does it feel to do everything right and have a child die?"

"Terrible. I was devastated. I think about Jamarr every day."

"Ms. Morris, is that because you feel personally responsible for the child's death?"

"No, but I am deeply saddened that this should happen to a child who I had worked with so closely."

"Ms. Morris, it must be convenient to blame your supervisors for this child's death. Is that what you're doing?"

"No. I am not blaming others. I have stated everything that I myself did . . . and I did everything that I could have . . . the system failed Jamarr."

Colon collects her thoughts. "Ms. Morris, just how did the system fail? You were the child's caseworker, you were closest to the child and his family. How can you blame the system?"

"As I have stated, I did everything that I should have done and I was refused at every turn. Jamarr died after I was taken off of the case."

"Ms. Morris, you have a Workman's Compensation suit for alleged mental health issues. What is that about?"

"I was devastated by Jamarr's death and then shocked again when the agency turned against me and blamed me for what happened."

"Ms. Morris, it sounds like you believe you failed the child. Did you fail Jamarr?"

"We all failed Jamarr. The agency failed Jamarr. His mother and grandmother failed him. I know in my heart that I did all that I could have done."

Colon is frustrated with her inability to crack me. Her tone is getting hostile. "Ms. Morris, you have an EEOC suit against DYFS, what is that about?"

"All of the supervisors were Latino and they received little or no discipline in this matter, whereas I was terminated."

"I see. The child was Latino, too. Was it his fault?"

"Ms. Colon, that's unfair and out of place," I answer.

"I apologize." Colon regathers herself. "So, you're suing your colleagues to shift the blame onto them?"

"No, I'm suing to stop the dangerous practice of treating Hispanic families differently when removing and returning children who are at high risk."

"So, Ms. Morris, your reasons are truly altruistic. Are you expecting financial compensation for this suit?"

"I only want these problems to be righted. The EEOC suit will hopefully accomplish that."

Colon is out of gas and exasperated. "No further questions."

I know I've done well. I told the truth and the truth supports everything I did to save Jamarr. My detractors shot themselves in the foot and the data is there to support that, despite their efforts to obfuscate and avoid it.

Pinarski agrees with my perception. "Kristin, you did great. Perfect. Under control, yet passionate and empathic . . . And, their testimony was gutted. Of course, one never knows about this sort of thing. At least it's not a jury . . . they are notoriously unpredictable."

"Thanks, I thought it went well," I say and smile weakly.

Pinarski continues, "A lot of times arbitrators try to average the findings, to apportion some of the blame to everyone involved. It's a mediation strategy. So, even if it goes your way, there still may be some penalty."

"Yeah," I sigh, "Over and above what I've been penalized already."

Pinarski nods knowingly.

I will have to wait for Tener's decision. I have no idea what he thinks about what he's heard . . . or how long he will take to issue his decision. I have no idea whether he must temper his decision in an effort to please everyone, or whether he is in a position to take a strong stance. My life is now in his hands.

Chapter 21

Olivia and Ellen testify after me, as does Christina, but I am not allowed to be present. In fact, an Administrative Assistant tells me that I must leave the building. However, I run into Ellen outside the New Jersey State House after her testimony.

"Kristin, I need to talk to you," Ellen says earnestly.

We walk together slowly, eyes to the ground, sometimes furtively scanning the area for people watching.

"You really need my report. It completely exonerates you from any wrong doing. I detail where Hilda, Christina, and others made their mistakes and I explicitly state 'That is where the punishment needs to be meted out.' Any way you can . . . get it; it shows everything."

"Ellen, I just want to thank you for what you did. It means everything to me. You're one of the very few who has the guts to do the right thing." I am so thankful.

"I don't know any other way. And . . . it's as clear as day."

"My attorneys fought to have it admitted, fighting a precedent in the State's position . . . but the judge would only let part of it in."

"They are really pushing to win this, at all costs," Ellen surmises.

Finally, the hearings are over. It is up to the arbitrator to sort through the morass of data . . . and bullshit.

Day by day I await Tener's decision in her arbitration case. One day while I'm at home folding clothes, the doorbell rings. I open the door for a courier, who curtly asks. "Kristin Morris?"

"Yes, that's me," I answer, wondering what could possibly come next. The courier hands me an envelope. "You've been served."

He turns and walks away, leaving me alone in the doorway. I stand motionless for a moment. I open the envelope, unfold the paper, and I am shocked by what I read. I close the door and lament to Benny.

"God help us . . . I'm being sued by Jamarr's mother. It's a civil suit against DYFS, its personnel . . . and me. I'm named in the suit. What am I going to do? Didn't she get enough money?"

"Oh my God. We have nothing left. She let the bastard back in her house and she's suing us? That bitch has no shame." Benny buries his face in his hands.

I search for some meaning in the situation. "The arbitration decision is due."

"Not soon enough! We've lost everything. This is not what I've worked for." Benny says, and I know he's right.

I call my attorneys. Anne Marie Pinarksi answers. I explain the situation. Unfortunately, I will have to obtain another union attorney paid for by the State for this lawsuit.

The days drag by. I know that this, too, will drag on interminably. I feel like I will never be free of litigation, of worry, of living in limbo.

Benny and I fight again. We become increasingly volatile.

"You sleep all the time! You do nothing around here! Now . . . you're being sued! What's next?!" Benny yells.

"I can't help it! I hate it! Who could have seen this coming?!"

"I never thought I'd be in this situation! We're losing everything! I'm not gonna live like this! I can't stand it! I can't take it!" he yells.

Cianna comes out of her bedroom in tears. "Stop fighting. Stop it, please . . . Daddy, you scream all the time."

I pick up our little girl. "She's right. It's getting worse and worse. It's not fair to the kids. I think you should move out."

"That's what you want? That's the solution?" Benny is floored.

"I think it's best for now. Stay at your mother's . . . see the children every day . . . come for dinner. I can't live like this either." I tell him. "I thought we were on the same side, Benny."

Benny goes to the bedroom and grabs a few things, glancing back with a pained look. He walks quietly out the door and starts his truck and drives away. Tears run down my cheeks. I hug Cianna in my lap.

Brian comes out of his room. He is shaken. "What happens now?"

"Brian, everything else stays the same. We live here and Dad visits when he wants. We'll try to work it out, it . . . it will just take time."

"Mom, all of this is because of your work. It doesn't seem worth it," Brian says.

I study him for a moment. "You're right . . . it's not."

"Why did this happen to you?" he asks.

"I don't know why. As you grow up, you'll see many things you won't understand. This is one I don't understand." I shrug my shoulders.

"Mommy, is something bad going to happen to someone else? Can other children get killed by their parents, too?" Cianna asks.

"Honey, all of you are safe. It will never happen here."

Cianna seems satisfied for now.

The cost of my decision is becoming overwhelming. To be true to oneself, to be courageous . . . this is something everyone believes they would want to do, and would be able to do. The cost is higher than I ever imagined.

I know in my heart that the State will probably settle the civil case, as that has been their pattern in the past. I consult with my new attorney, Mr. Matthew Behr of Marshall, Dennehey, Warner, Coles, Colin, and Ciggio, appointed by the State of New Jersey to defend me.

Behr introduces himself and explains, "I'm your lawyer, but I still represent the State."

Since no decision has been reached in my arbitration hearing, I am clearly at risk for being found guilty in a civil suit. My attorney gives me information that doesn't surprise me. There are other instances of incorrect case management based on children's Latino ethnicity.

Then, I learns facts I hadn't prepared myself for. Mr. Behr reads from the City of Camden Police report and the Prosecutors' Office. Omayra Cruz knew Jamarr was in serious danger long before the emergency call. Jamarr was coughing up blood and she gave him chicken soup and put him to bed. If she had acted more quickly, he might have been saved. I am overwhelmed. It morphs into a horror story. I didn't even get the truth about Jamarr's death . . . and he suffered needlessly longer. Williams admitted to systematically torturing Jamarr in ways that avoided detection. The fatal beating was Williams stomping him in the abdomen. There were at least twenty beatings before that, with the injuries inflicted in places nobody would see.

I am hysterical. Tears come to Behr's eyes as he reads. I ask him to stop. I can't take it. It was bad enough without the graphic details.

I recognize that the State will do whatever it has to do, as it always does, to cover for itself. The investigation uncovers the misguided Latino loyalty, but everything will be kept under wraps. Most disconcerting is the knowledge that resolution will be at some unforeseeable time in my already uncertain future. Behr advises me to pursue the EEOC suit based on his purview of the situation. I get the impression that he knows the full scope of events, but he sticks to the job at hand, defending me in the civil suit.

The same holds true for my EEOC suit with The Pearce Law Firm. The monetary figures the State of New Jersey has offered are ludicrously low. The Workman's Comp case feels like it will never happen. It is hard to fathom the motives for this type of behavior. Time continues. I live in limbo. I am forever on the edge of hell, but not in hell itself.

Chapter 22

At the state house conference room for the arbitration decision, Jeffrey Tener announces his findings to me, my attorneys, the State's attorneys, Christina Moses, and Union reps. Everyone sits quietly with expectant looks.

Tener speaks in an official and authoritative tone. "I have the opinion in this Matter of Binding Arbitration, The State of New Jersey vs. Kristin Morris."

"The State terminated Morris, the employee with the least experience and responsibility and issued no discipline to others. Morris had no prior record of any disciplinary infractions."

Tener looks around and pauses. "The facts indicate that Morris made the Required Monthly Visits and documented those visits."

My attorneys' faces brighten a little.

"Morris did not sign the document at the supervisory conference of October twenty-third, two-thousand nine when the case was closed despite high-risk level. Not only did Morris not sign the document, she had no access to it in the computer system."

Tener clears his throat. "When Morris was presented with this document by her supervisor, she refused to sign it."

Colon starts to look concerned. Tener sounds slightly angered as he continues. "Morris and Figueroa made efforts to have the child removed in September two-thousand nine which is well supported in the record. It is not accurate that Morris did nothing or ignored red flags."

I see Pinarski glance at Richardson with a slight smile.

"Morris followed up and informed Robinson from her car immediately after the visit and wanted the child removed. Morris and Figueroa returned to their office and immediately began required background checks for removal to the home of a relative. Morris did exactly what Moses said she should have done; she sought a Dodd removal."

Tener pauses for a moment to review his notes. "Morris and Robinson did everything they could to protect the child. In a last ditch effort, Morris called the hot line to report abuse the child had reported and requested an emergency visit. Feliciano investigated and concluded there had been no abuse, the child was safe, and no safety plan was needed. Consequently, DYFS could not provide any services."

Nicole Colon looks down as Pinarski and Richardson focus on her.

Tener concludes. "Morris went to Robinson after Feliciano's conclusions and made the case again for the removal of the child only to be told that the case must be closed and nothing could be done. Morris asked to visit the child again and Robinson refused to allow it. The State cannot reasonably expect Morris to have done any more."

Small beads of sweat show on Colon's brow as she starts to gather her papers together for a quick retreat. This makes me smile.

Tener speaks with forceful authority. "Morris is found blameless on all counts. The State is directed to reinstate Morris and to make her whole in all respects including salary, benefits, and seniority. This meeting is adjourned."

DYFS personnel exit quickly without comment. Tener shakes my hand and says, "Thank you, for your patience and courage."

"Thank you, Mr. Tener." I am beaming.

Tenet shakes hands with Richardson, and Pinarski and exits the room.

Pinarski embraces me. "This is unprecedented . . . this has never happened in the history of DYFS. Complete exoneration," she says.

"Congratulations!" Richardson says and hugs me.

"God is good," is all I manage to say.

Less than an hour later, I call Dr. Zielinski to tell him the good news. He is busy with a patient, but I leave a message with Karen.

I celebrate with my family. I am overjoyed and ready to return to work. Being true to myself has paid off. Benny and I talk every day and he is happy for me. We are healing more and more.

Chapter 23

One week later, I walk in for therapy, crestfallen. Dr. Zielinski is taken aback by my sad demeanor, expecting a celebratory meeting. He quickly adjusts and greets me somberly.

I walk in and sit down. "The arbitration was for nothing . . . a total waste of time. My lawyer, Anne Marie Pinarski, called. She said that the State was going to fight tooth and nail for the arbitration money I won, and worse. They won't take me back to work. It makes no sense. I was completely exonerated! How can this be? How can they do this?"

Dr. Zielinski hands me a box of tissues. "How can they go against the arbitration?" he asks.

"They're offering a so-called global settlement . . . combining the EEOC and Workman's Comp suits. But that doesn't even cover my back wages. All on the condition that I permanently resign. They won't let me come back to work."

"You're kidding me. What's the issue? What're they afraid of?"

"Supposedly, if I were to get future disciplinary action, I could use it in a retaliation suit against them. Which is totally bogus. It took all this time to overturn this and they don't want me back. I did everything I could do to prove myself."

"This is bullshit. Kristin, you're the kind of person they should want on their team. You were the only person between Jamarr and his fate. You defended him fiercely again and again and again. They not only ignored you, they ran over you. Then they buried their mistakes, just like they buried the child . . . now they want to bury you."

"I know you're right. They perjured themselves, tampered with witnesses, withheld records, and I still won. They never expected I would overturn the case. Now, they don't want me back. That's the biggest slap in the face."

"Anne Marie Pinarski has made multiple calls to all of the involved personnel. Colon, the opposing lawyer, wouldn't return her calls. She worked her way up the chain of command of DYFS to Human Resources. I keep calling her, but she has no answers for me, and she hasn't gotten anything from them . . . only that they want this global settlement thing."

"Who do they think they are?! They did all of those crooked things, and no consequences." Dr. Zielinski is in disbelief.

"Apparently, no one is over them. They stole my life. What employer would ever believe this story and hire me now? And Yolanda is still angry with me. She was demoted and was docked pay. She feels like I threw her under the bus . . . but all I did was tell the truth."

Dr. Zielinski summarizes. "She was bullied and pressured, too. But let me guess, nothing has happened to the supervisors who forced these decisions."

"No, nothing."

"You're expendable. The question is why? Someone is covering up for some big reasons." There is a long pause.

"This just goes on and on, doesn't it?" I shake my head.

"Apparently, that's their strategy. You have to take this over for yourself."

"Ellen Finley, the auditor who wouldn't lie for them . . . she is encouraging me not to give up, to fight it." I have a realization. "I depended on the system. It doesn't work. I'm ready. You know, I still think writing a book would be a good idea, but I'd need your help."

"That's an option," Dr. Zielinski says. "I mean, what is binding arbitration supposed to mean? I might make some phone calls to inquire about all this."

I give him my permission. I need all the help I can get.

———————————

During our next visit, Dr. Zielinski tells me he called the Federal Monitor.

"I called Judith Meltzer's office and actually got ahold of her. I told her that they weren't letting you back to work after winning the arbitration, and even though she recognized your name and wondered what had happened to you, all she said was 'I don't get involved with personnel issues.' When I mentioned the settled lawsuit in which Omayra Cruz was given $425,000.00, Melzer said, 'I thought settling that was a good idea.' And, when I asked her about Latino ethnic influences on case management decision, she said, 'She didn't know anything about that.' She even fed me some numbers about how DYFS has improved since 2006." He's clearly annoyed, but I'm not surprised at Meltzer's response.

"Well, thank you for trying," I say.

"Then, I got notice that my food stamps and Medicaid benefits will be cut off."

"Wait a minute. How did that happen?" he asks.

"They share the same system. They know that I was ordered back to work by the arbitrator."

"No, Tener's decision was on paper. Someone had to deliberately go into the state program, follow the prompts, look for your name, key in the changes, hit the submit buttons. They're out to get you . . . they're not letting you back to work, but they're treating your benefits as if you are back at work. This is outright corruption and conspiracy."

"You think it's deliberate?"

"I'm positive . . . they're out to break you financially." Dr. Zielinski looks at me with concern. "This can't be coincidence. Someone with power is behind this. Look, they've isolated you and forced you into a passive, waiting position. The whole sequence of events has been defined by them. Kristin, you need to take a more aggressive position . . . go public. Public opinion would be outraged." He pauses. "Let's think this through. Fear is driving this. There is more fear than power in their actions. The whole damn mess was driven by fear, not strength or integrity. What are they really afraid of? It's got to be exposure."

He collects his thoughts. "In addition, they're trying to make the child protection system look better than it is, and you know too much."

"You're right," I say, starting to see how the pieces fit. "Yeah, my civil suit settled with Jamarr's mother for four hundred and twenty-five thousand dollars. They didn't want to risk a trial that would publicly expose the pattern of differential treatment of Latino families."

"Great . . . with the other millions she got. But it proves the point. They're looking to avoid any bad press . . . and they're willing to pay to avoid it," says Dr. Zielinski. "With your permission, I'd like to write a letter to the Governor's Office of Constituent Relations on your behalf."

I ask for a copy of the letter. This is what it said:

CHAPTER TWENTY-THREE

Dear Honorable Governor Christie,

As a constituent, I am compelled to bring to your attention the situation of Kristin Morris, a Camden Division DYFS caseworker who is experiencing the worst miscarriage of justice that I have ever personally encountered. Ms. Morris resides in Blackwood, NJ, Camden County.

On March 31st, 2009 in Camden, NJ, Jamarr Cruz, a nine-year-old boy, was murdered by his mother's boyfriend, Vince Williams. What happened after that is likely the biggest cover up in DYFS history.

Vince Williams had already been incarcerated before for severely beating Jamarr. Upon his release from prison, Jamarr's mother, Omayra Cruz, welcomed him back into her home where he proceeded to abuse Jamarr again.

Kristin Morris was the Camden Division DYFS caseworker assigned to Jamarr's case. Six months earlier, Ms. Morris fought heroically to block Jamarr's return to his mother after he had been put into foster care with his grandmother. Ms. Morris was overruled time and time again by her Latino supervisors whose loyalty to their own rigid ideas about Latino families was more important than protecting the safety of an innocent child. Case management decisions differentially based on a family's racial or cultural ties represent a pattern in the Camden Division and perhaps other offices throughout New Jersey.

After Jamarr's death, Kristin was scapegoated and blamed for his death and given the option of a twenty-day suspension versus termination. Ms. Morris refused the suspension, knowing that she did nothing wrong and had fiercely fought to get

Jamarr removed from his mother's care. This led to termination from her job with subsequent arbitration hearings that dragged on for over two years. In the meantime, Omayra Cruz was given millions of dollars in hush money, his grandmother was given lesser amounts, and maybe Jamarr's biological father (who only knew Jamarr for the first six months of his life and was then incarcerated for child molestation and released from prison just six months before Jamarr's murder) was also given hush money by some unknown source.

During the binding arbitration hearings, DYFS high officials kept key data from being exposed (e.g., Ms. Finley's auditor's records; although Ms. Finley testified), two witnesses were tampered with via supervisor threats, and some of the upper management in DYFS perjured themselves. Despite these irregularities, the arbitrator, Mr. Jeffrey Tener, exonerated Ms. Morris on each and every accusation and he implicitly placed the blame for Jamarr's death on Kristin's supervisors. To date, they have received no punishment.

This is the first time in DYFS history that an individual has been completely exonerated. DYFS was directed to return Ms. Morris to her prior employment without loss of seniority and benefits and with back pay. DYFS and certain State officials in the executive branch have deliberately ignored and opposed this decision made under so called "binding arbitration." They are contending that Ms. Morris might use any future disciplinary action of her as an accusation in a retaliation suit. Ms. Laurie Hodian appears to be the current decision maker, although others preceded her, most notably during the last gubernatorial election. The former Governor was apparently concerned about DYFS bad press during the last gubernato-

rial election and hushed the situation at that time.

Ms. Morris loves her job as a DYFS caseworker. She has never had any disciplinary actions against her in her six years with the department. Furthermore, her handling of Jamarr's case could be used as a teaching model for future cases. Ms. Morris has been out of work for three years now. She can't get food stamps or Medicaid and her house is in foreclosure because, according to the arbitrator, she should be back at work. So the State of New Jersey has cut her off from such benefits. What future employer would believe this story as to why Ms. Morris has been out of work and hire her? For all practical purposes, she is unemployable. All the while, Jamarr's mother is sitting in the lap of luxury spending her millions to help her mourn the death of her son. Something is terribly wrong here.

Is this not an obvious travesty of justice? Ms. Morris tried desperately to remove Jamarr from harm's way and DYFS superiors wouldn't see fit to tarnish a minority's ethnic pride. So a young boy dies senselessly, the mother is rewarded monetarily, and the caseworker blocked from doing her job properly is losing her home. DYYFS is trying to quiet her about this situation by accepting a so called "global settlement." They have offered a lowball financial figure which includes Ms. Morris' permanent resignation from DYFS. In other words, she must give up her career to receive the money.

Ultimately, Ms. Morris would like to see the system work properly so there are no more "Jamarr Cruz" tragedies. She wants to return to her career doing work that few of us could or would want to do.

Our legislators are unlikely to know about this situation

as this has occurred within DYFS and the executive branch of state government. Parenthetically, Omayra Cruz, Jamarr's mother, has initiated a civil suit against DYFS, which will probably be "settled" in the next year or two due to DYFS's fear of negative publicity. As a citizen of New Jersey, I ask that you and your legislative colleagues investigate this matter, explore case management decisions that are based on ethnicity rather than the merits of a case, make all of this a matter of public knowledge and concern, determine where the hush money came from, publicize Ms. Cruz's shameless lawsuit, and explore why Ms. Morris is being treated in this fashion.

In short, an interested observer might get the impression of both criminal activity and malfeasance in office.

Respectfully,
Joseph J. Zielinski, Ph.D.

Dr. Zielinski also faxes a copy of the letter to a Ms. Marcia Lowry, a children's rights activist, whom he discovered while looking up the origin of the Federal Monitor situation in New Jersey. His research led him to the very public case of the Jackson children who were found to be eating out of garbage cans while in foster care in Collingswood, New Jersey in 2003. Marcia Robinson Lowry initiated and led the lawsuit against the State of New Jersey as an Executive Director of Children's Rights in New York City back in 1999. Another agency, A Better Childhood, was also involved.

Several weeks later, Dr. Zielinski tells me that he got a call from the Governor's Office saying they received the letter. However, they couldn't speak to him because they don't have a release to do so. Also, because there is pending litigation, they can't speak to him about the situation.

"I asked them if they would speak to you, and they said they would call you," Dr. Zielinski finishes.

"They did call me," I say. "They told me the same: they couldn't speak to me because there is pending litigation. Look, I really appreciate all your efforts. But they will keep finding loopholes to avoid helping me against the State." I look down at the floor. I feel deflated.

"It seems that way," Dr. Zielinski says. "But we can't give up."

Another week passes. There has been no reply from Marcia Lowry. Dr. Zielinski e-mails her again. He adds, "Please let me know that you read this, even if you are unable to do anything about it."

An hour later he receives an e-mail reply from Ms. Lowry. "It would not be appropriate for me to become involved in this situation."

No one wants to get involved. Everyone has their reasons not to. No one seems to care about Jamarr Cruz's death, the injustice done to me, or the possibility that other Latino children may be at risk. Everything is a dead end. The bureaucracy is seamless without an apparent chink in their armor. Are people afraid, or just indifferent? Over time, it is becoming clear that an interlocking series of people and situations have coalesced into a barrier that is impervious to disassembling.

Chapter 24

Life at home has been difficult as well. Benny has been taking any and all side jobs to keep food on the table. We have been talking, even seeing each other almost daily for dinner and to play with our children. One evening he shows up with flowers.

"Kristin, I want to come home. I want to move back in with you and the kids. I want to keep our family together," he says.

"Ok," I say, smiling. "Let's get through this together." I hug Benny tightly, thankful for my family and my husband.

At my next meeting with Dr. Zielinski, I tell him the good news. "Well, my husband and I are working things out. I'm really happy about that." I heave a big sigh. "But, the home foreclosure papers finalized this week. We have ten days to get out."

"Wow, I'm sorry to hear about the house," Dr. Zielinski says.

"In the meantime, I'm not getting any press, any recognition, anything." I trail off. "How come whenever I ask you about helping me to write a book, you ignore me?"

Dr. Zielinski clears his throat and I wonder if I've made him uncomfortable by pressing the issue.

"You're right. I have. But I have been thinking about it. It's way out of the norm for what therapists do. It's considered a 'dual relationship' and it can create problems for both of us. Yet, you're clearly not getting anywhere with the usual avenues. We've tried everything. I don't know what's left. We can try to write a book."

"Yes. Thank you! Anything you can do without spending too much time," I say.

<hr />

The foreclosure on our home is complete; we move out with the help of some of our friends.

After we finish for the day, we thank our friends and they go home. Benny's Ford pickup is stacked with boxes next to a rental truck. I stare at our packed-up life.

"We're homeless . . . ruined. I can't believe it turned out like this," I say.

"Kristin, we'll start over. We're young. We can do it." Benny tries to be positive.

"All I wanted was to do the right thing."

"You did everything right," he assures me.

My father brings the kids back home. Moving boxes line the walls.

"I'll put the kids to bed," Benny says, leaving my father and I sitting at the kitchen table.

"The school will let the kids stay 'til the end of the school year," I say, looking for a silver lining to all this. Then I break. "Dad, the State is starving us out. The union failed. My lawyers failed. I'm starting to get pressure to settle in the EEOC suit. They want it over and the State is not acting in good faith . . . not that they ever did. The figures are ridiculous."

"Kristin, there are conflicts of interest all over the place. I can't stand to see what this is doing to you. You need to blow this thing out of the water by going public. It's time."

"You're right. There's nothing left to lose."

"I'll help you. Tell them they have a brief time window for a just resolution . . . then we go to the media. These manipulators need to be exposed for what they are."

"It's settled. I'll do it."

In the following weeks we are proactive. My father writes a letter to DCPP with our stipulations. Not surprisingly, it falls on deaf ears. We try to contact multiple newspapers, talk shows, exposé forums, but no one gets back to us. It probably takes a professional to do this effectively. But we don't have the money, and we don't have the experience. It's almost like the State knew this would be the case.

Chapter 25

I have been waking up nauseous for a few days. Then, my period is late. I do a home pregnancy test and there is a little plus sign on the stick. It is positive.

That night I sit Benny down. "I'm ninety-nine percent sure I'm pregnant," I tell him.

Tears of joy come to Benny's eyes. "Oh my God! Honey, this is wonderful."

We had not planned to have more children, but this is a blessing. With all that has been going on in our lives, a baby will be a wonderful and exciting gift.

Several weeks pass and I decide to tell Dr. Zielinski. I call him, as I have been so busy and hampered by Workman's Compensation IMEs that I haven't been in for any therapy sessions in a while.

"Dr. Z . . . I'm pregnant."

"Kristin, that's great! How are you feeling?"

"Not bad . . . actually pretty good."

"You should go off all of your medications and tell Dr. Rosenberg that you're pregnant," he advises me.

"It's OK. I haven't had the money to purchase the medications . . . Workman's Comp is refusing to pay."

"OK, good. But keep in touch and keep seeing Dr. Rosenberg as your pregnancy continues. Mood changes can occur. After the baby is born, you have to watch postpartum with your history."

"Yeah, thanks. I will. The kids are calling. I have to go now."

"Take care . . . and keep in touch, OK?"

Chapter 26

I receive a strange and unexpected phone call from a DCPP Human Resources person, Linda Lebron.

Linda begins, "Kristin Morris?"

"Yes, this is Kristin."

"Linda Lebron from HR. We are scheduling you to return to work. You need to come to Trenton tomorrow for finger printing and processing. You're to be back at work on Monday."

"OK . . . ?" I respond uncertainly, understandably wary.

"Good. You'll be required to attend the New Worker Training classes. We hold them in Newark and Parsippany."

"But I've done these three times already . . . I have six years of experience in the field, and I'm pregnant."

"You'll have to do the required training work. There's no choice in the matter," Linda replies curtly.

"Of course."

"OK, we'll get you on the schedule. The next class starts a week from this Monday. Goodbye."

I am thrilled, bewildered and angry, all at once. What's their angle? Why do I have to drive all over the state for training I already have? But I don't have a choice.

When I begin the training, it is a total waste of time, as I expected. It is all a review of the years of experience I have under my belt. I commute four hours roundtrip per day for several days. They may have mentioned the turnpike in a song or two, but there is nothing romantic about it.

However, I give birth to Vienna, an eight pound, healthy baby girl, providing a welcome break to the tedium of driving mindless miles. Benny cries so hard from joy. I have never seen him cry like that. Our little girl will never know what we have been through.

After my maternity leave, I prepare myself for more useless commuting. I put in a complaint to my union rep with the context of having a new baby. The State actually relents and agrees to send a teacher down to southern New Jersey. It becomes rapidly clear that I know more than the teacher, who has never been in the field. Marvin is a good teacher, but his knowledge is primarily book-based. Because of my participation and commentary on the very first day, Marvin realizes that he doesn't need to be there.

"Kristin, it's clear that you already know this material. I don't even know why you're here. Let me see if I can get you excused from the rest of it. No reason to waste your time. You simply don't need this."

"Thanks. Anything you can do with that will be great."

"No really, you're telling me things, practical things, that I didn't know." He shakes his head. "My field experience is limited. You're giving me another view. You could teach this class."

"Hey, can I have your boss's number . . . maybe there's a job for me in your department." We both laugh. I have not completely lost my sense of humor.

I am formally returned to work at DCPP in August 2012 and assigned to the Gloucester County Division Office, during which time frame I attended the New Workers' Training. The surprise call from Human Resources occurred months after Dr. Zielinski's letter to Governor Christie, but no one knows for sure if the letter had anything to do with it.

The day I start, I am met by a union official, Sean Lugwig, which is less than comforting, as he had been close with Hilda and Christina. I wonder if I can trust him. Sean had worked under Hilda Vega for years. Hilda was his casework supervisor. No undue influence here. Is this the network at play? As it turned out, Sean wasn't even allowed inside the room to hear what transpired.

At the initial meeting, Allison Blake, a Human Resources person, shows up and informs me that at work, "Nothing is to be said or spoken about with regard to your situation. We are referring to it as a simple 'worker transfer.' No one is to speak about your situation."

After Allison leaves, San Payne, the Office Manager, enters the room and introduces herself. She says, "Kristin, I know what happened. You have a clean slate here."

"My slate was never dirty. I was completely exonerated," I say a bit snappily.

"Let's just get you together. I bought some bagels. Just hand them out and we'll introduce you. Remember, don't speak about your situation."

With a worker transfer, the person just shows up and is informally introduced to the staff. A special introductory meeting with bagels is neither usual nor customary. Everyone will know it's for show.

My new colleagues enter the room. I hand out the bagels. One worker asks me, "Where you coming from?"

"Camden office," I say. I look around the room and I know that they know.

Later, as I move about the office, I can tell that the other workers are talking about me. Why wouldn't they? Already on this new assignment my past becomes an underlying backdrop of stress that pervades everything I do. No one knows it, but I carry Tener's arbitration report on my person at all times, just in case someone confronts me about what happened.

A week into my time at the Gloucester County Office, Sean Lugwig asks me how I'm doing. I express my doubts.

"Do you have a job?" Sean asks sarcastically.

"Yes."

"That's all that matters."

I come to learn that in the Gloucester office, people are fired for all kinds of flimsy reasons. One woman was on medical leave for cancer was fired and killed herself soon after. No one knew if it was despondency due to her cancer, the harshness of her firing, or maybe both.

To add insult to injury, I am seated for several weeks in the Transportation Aides' section of the office, another factor making me feel like an outsider.

Later I am reassigned to a disorganized supervisor, whose morbid obesity interferes with her mobility and office organization. I am confronted with fifteen cases of total chaos, with paperwork on each littered about the office. This supervisor is lazy. Totally overwhelmed, I begin to panic and luckily, several clerical workers come in to help me organize the mess. The cases still don't line up on their time lines. Since they are now my cases, I am accountable for their handling. The pressure starts to mount. I begin to experience flashbacks of memories with Jamarr.

Then, I am assigned to another supervisor, Denise Mateo. I am initially concerned, as Denise is married to Daniel Garcia, the caseworker who was going to close the Pena case, back when things first started to unravel for me. However, Denise turns out to be an excellent supervisor with whom I work well.

In the break room one day, Mada, a Latino worker, blurts out, "So, what's your deal?"

"Nothing." I say, trying to follow the directive to say nothing.

"I heard you got knocked up by a Puerto Rican," Mada responds.

"You mean my husband of sixteen years?!" Everybody thinks they know everything.

A week later, Carmen, a litigation specialist approaches me. "Can I talk to you?" She motions to the ladies' room.

Carmen wastes no time. "Do you have a lawsuit against the State?" she asks.

I am momentarily shocked into silence.

Carmen continues, "I know everything . . . You're not going to be here for long. I've heard the back room discussion. 'Don't give her a permanent seat.'" Carmen studies me. "Workers are sent here to be gotten rid of."

I remain silent, taking it all in.

"Look, I know how these people can be. Susan, the administrative assistant, she just coordinates everything."

I begin to cry silently.

Carmen finishes, "Actually, everybody knows everything. They talk about it all the time."

A few days later, a coworker confers with me in an isolated hallway. "Kristin, you need to know something about why they sent you here. This is where they send workers they want to fire. There's a pattern that's impossible to miss."

Again I am shocked. "I don't know what to say. I was surprised that they even brought me back, but I had no idea it was to set me up."

The coworker continues, "Look, I can't say too much, but the Office Manager here is looking to advance herself as fast as possible. She's already moved up by playing by the division's rules, if you catch my drift. Watch your back. I can't be seen hanging out with you." She walks away.

I stand in the hallway clueless and forlorn.

I am given many cases very quickly, purportedly to lighten the load on my overworked colleagues. I am given as many as ten high-risk cases over and above the agency guidelines of six or seven. I quickly find myself working sixty hours per week, and struggling after hours to keep up with the paperwork. I am so frightened of making a mistake that I double check everything, increasing my work time.

Another coworker spontaneously speaks to me in the otherwise unoccupied ladies' room one day. "I feel sorry for you. We all do. You have the toughest caseload in this office. We don't know how you're doing it."

"I don't know how I'm doing it either . . . or even if I can continue to maintain this pace . . . this workload."

The coworker continues, "You should at least talk to San to let her know your concerns and then . . . document your meetings."

"Thanks for the heads up. I was thinking about speaking to her, but I was warned that she's generally unresponsive."

"You're right, but create a paper trail."

"I've done that before . . . and I can do it again . . . but it doesn't always work."

Another worker enters the ladies' room, so we stop speaking and exit.

When I bring my workload issue to the attention of San, I am given blanket assurance that I am doing a good job.

"San, I have more cases than anyone and too many high-risk cases."

"Kristin, you're an experienced worker. You're doing fine. We brought you here to help reduce the overload. Hang in there. It will even out."

"But I'm working way too many hours and it's affecting my home life," I say.

San finishes. "Look, I have to go now. This job affects all of our home lives." She walks away.

One day at lunch in the conference room, I sit with other workers.

They look at me and the room goes silent.

One of them asks, "Well . . . are you going to tell us what happened?"

Finally, the cat will come out of the bag. I collect my thoughts. I take a deep breath and begin to tell my story. The entire room is aghast as the details emerge. They all realize that it could have happened to them. Although everyone had been talking about it, and everyone thought they knew everything, they didn't.

When I finish, one of my colleagues, Michelle, gasps, "Oh my God!" These people are not part of it. They can't be on my side, but they are not against me. The decision makers, whoever they are, call the shots.

At my next therapy session, I tell Dr. Zielinski about everything happening at work.

"It looks like they are trying to break you . . . either force you to resign, or set you up for a mistake. It's the same old story. All we have to do is wait for their next maneuvers."

"I wanted to go back to work, but not like this. Not with the new baby and all. Benny's worried about me, and he's upset that I'm not there for the kids again. I don't want to repeat history." I pause and becomes tearful. "Vienna bonded with Benny. I was gone all day into the evening. Yeah, he's her father. But it hurts . . . if she's upset, or hurt, or scared, she reaches for him."

"This job is totally sucking everything out of you. Who wants to do this kind of work? Really, Kristin, it's not worth giving up your life," Dr. Zielinski says.

"For right now, we have no choice. We need my income."

Dr. Zielinski is still sympathetic, but firm. "I hate to give you more work than you have, but you have to document everything.

Maybe even go over the office director's head by copying everything you send to San."

"I am documenting all of it. But copying . . . I hadn't thought of it. My hesitation is that she's doing this based on direction from above. The word is that she advanced so fast because she plays ball with the bosses."

"The problem is the people in control. They need to be deposed from their little fiefdoms . . . one way or the other. I dream about it," Dr. Zielinski says.

"You dream about it. I live it. Once again, the question is how?"

If their plan is to wait for me to mess up so that can fire me, I just have to be careful. No slip-ups, no changes in my case management pattern, nothing they can fault me on.

The work situation itself would be more than most anyone could deal with effectively, but there is the lingering litigation, and there is my personal life on top of it.

I asked Mr. Ringland, my EEOC attorney, if he could glean any semblance of a reason for their desire to get rid of me, and who specifically wanted it.

Ringland replied, "The best they would offer is that it's like having a girlfriend you broke up with . . . You don't want her around. And they refuse to offer anything on who's behind this."

"Really, like an old girlfriend. I was a professional doing my job. and I did it right! An old girlfriend?!"

Ringland is also disgusted. "Yeah, it's ridiculous. But we'll never know for sure what this is really about. And the money they're offering—pitiful, and only if you resign."

"I don't want to resign," I say firmly. The State's position is so deeply dug in, there must be stakeholders behind this. Who are they?

I continue to do my job to the best of my abilities, which are considerable. I am assigned cases about to be formally closed with home situations so bad that I have to remove the children. During this time, I remove so many endangered children from their homes that I am nicknamed "the Dodd Queen." I encounter no resistance as there is a very small Hispanic population in Gloucester County and almost all of these removals are from non-Latino families. At the same time, I question my judgment to the extent that I frequently bounce situations off of a few trusted colleagues for their input.

Chapter 27

Even though it's my lawsuit, I am not invited into the actual EEOC arbitration meetings. My two attorneys, Judith Pearce and William Ringland, go in with a team of five to six people from the State of New Jersey, including attorneys from the Department of Law and the Attorney General's office. Sometimes it is only Mr. Ringland. The negotiations almost come to resolution, but my attorneys and I won't accept the amount offered by the State.

At the beginning of each day, whether in the small waiting room, during lunch breaks in the small lunch area, or at the end of each day's meeting, I sit with my attorneys. The State's attorneys never look at me, even when my adversaries sit and eat a few feet away. They refrain from even looking in my direction upon entering and leaving the room. I stare at them consistently to the point that my own attorneys notice and comment on it. But the opposing lawyers do not entertain my stares. At first I wonder how they could be so cold, but I realize that they can not bear to deal with me as a person. I am not a person, not a human being, not a mother and wife, not a top-notch case worker. No, I am a number and a money figure. The State's lawyers can't do their job effectively if they have to deal with the humanity of one Kristin Morris. They would like nothing more than if I were to disappear. That is what the State of New Jersey has wanted all along . . . and I simply won't go away.

Soon I experience pressure from my attorneys. My EEOC attorney, Mr. Ringland, reads the proposed settlement to me and interprets it for me, minimizing some of the stipulations. This settlement not only includes my permanent future resignation from DCPP, but also blocks my vesting in the pension plan. Ringland implies that I could apply for a job with DCPP at some later time and they would never know. But I don't believe him. My whole career would be over.

Both Benny and I are out of work, our house is foreclosed on, and I have been softened up by the punishing, erosive influence of time. In a moment of weakness due to battle fatigue, I agree and sign the settlement. I immediately regret my decision and the next day I am hysterical. I feel like I have sold my soul to the devil. But it is too late. The deal is done. At least I am out of the hell hole at Gloucester City. That was a disaster waiting to happen. At the same time, my Office Manager of that time, Amanda Hammond, and her Supervisor, Denise Mateo, cry at losing me. They know that I was doing my job for the kids and their well-being. I am a mess.

Still, I have a personal life and financial problems. The EEOC case settles. The settlement of two hundred and fifty thousand is reduced by legal costs and the forty percent contingency fee. I walk away with one hundred and twenty-five thousand, which isn't even close to my past wages. In retrospect, I see how the State wages its war of attrition. My law firm continued to amass legal fees without reimbursement which mathematically continued to reduce their profit with the contingency fee. They see the State not making truly legitimate offers, so they must cut their losses, and mine, too. They just don't appreciate the cost to my soul this Pyrrhic victory exacts.

Only later do I read the fine print. The lifetime agreement to separate from DCPP includes all vendors and social agencies with which DCPP contracts. This was minimized by my attorneys. I send out over fifty resumes and get "not qualified" responses to companies offering thirteen dollars an hour. Either they didn't read my resume, or something else is going on. I go to an interview in Philadelphia in Pennsylvania's DHS system. I get three interviews, and one goes so well I feel confident I will get the position. I get no offers. Was I being blackballed? How far reaching are the State of New Jersey's tentacles?

I never forgot Sally, one of my former clients, now a young woman with a child of her own. I remember her as the fourteen-year-old girl who wore her heart on her sleeve even though her youth had been wasted in the foster care system her entire life. She cared for her two younger siblings and wanted above all else to keep her family together. She even refused an adoption opportunity that would not keep her with her siblings . . . and she really loved her mother. Sally was always respectful. She was a great student who was into drama and performed in school plays.

I was able to get Sally and her brother together in the same foster home and Sally began to let her guard down enough to trust me. Later, I helped arrange an adoption with an extended family member with one of her brothers, a placement that allowed her other brother and her mother continued contact with her new family. I did all I could to support Sally emotionally, even going to her plays and visiting her after her case was transferred to another worker. I promised to attend her graduation and kept that promise in my mind and heart. I always kept my promises. But then, Jamarr was murdered and I was out of work and worried that it would be chancy to keep visiting Sally. I feared getting into more trouble and visiting that grief upon Sally's family. Sally and I lost contact for five years.

I wanted to somehow make good on my promise and so I searched for Sally. I was delighted to find her. We began to talk through Facebook.

Sally confided, "You could never know how much you changed my life . . . what kind of impact you made on me. At a time when I hated my family, you made me feel loved."

I was uncomfortably embarrassed, but at the same time, it was the best feeling in the world. Coming on the trail of accusations of professional neglect and incompetence, it brought me to tears.

"You gave me hope that I was not alone in the world. Someone was out there looking out for me. You may not have known it, but I have never forgotten what you did for me," Sally confided. "I can't believe what they did to you. I know you're the best . . . and to be treated like that."

"Thank you . . . and thank you for allowing me to reach out to you. I remember your situation. I never know how I'm being perceived . . . the only way I know is to do my best," I replied to her.

Now, at least I know that all of my efforts were not in vain. I have made a difference in others' lives. How many more Sallys are out there? I will never know. I may never get the chance to do this work again.

I become increasingly despondent. I have no career and no future. This has been wrongly taken from me. My anxiety is even worse as I contemplate my lack of direction. Yet, I am grateful and thankful for my children and family.

I fantasize about starting a nonprofit organization for abused children. I would provide all of the needed services with a group of dedicated professionals under the umbrella of an excellent foster care facility. I have become cynical in a way I have never been. How can so many people succumb to the maintenance of injustice? I have now come to believe in the concept of evil in the world . . . along with complacency and fear. The State of New Jersey wants me gone.

Chapter 28

During my next therapy session, Dr. Zielinski tells me of his own troubles with the State of New Jersey. We suspect these problems are a result of the letter Dr. Zielinski wrote to the governor when trying to help me. He receives official correspondence from the New Jersey Division of Taxation informing him that he owes $1600 on his 2014 taxes. He pulls out his personal tax file and quickly sees that they did not credit him with a significant overpayment from 2013 which he assigned forward to the 2014 tax due.

Dr. Zielinski tries for several days to call the Division of Taxation, but the phone message repeatedly informs him that they can't take his call due to "high demand." After two weeks, he elects to call the Governor's Office. He explains his situation and, to his surprise, he is immediately patched through to the Division of Taxation.

The Division rep takes a minute to review his account and informs him, "The problem is that you didn't file your taxes in 2011 and 2012."

"Yes, I did. I'm always on top of this." Dr. Zielinski is shocked and irritated.

The rep continues, "Well, we have no record of having received them. I would advise you to send them in immediately, so we can begin to sort through this."

Dr. Zielinski agrees and hangs up thinking this will be a nuisance, but something he will easily clear up. He sends in the requested returns and soon finds out that the State's Division of Taxation stamped his just sent returns with the receipt date of July 31st, more than three years past the original due date. He is informed that this is to be his initial filing date and by state statute, they will not credit him with substantial overpayments for each missing year, of $2900 plus and $2500 plus, respectively. Since he elects to roll overpayments toward next year's tax liability, the State will not credit these overpayments, which leaves Dr. Zielinski with a debt, including interest and penalties.

Dr. Zielinski is furious and he writes a letter outlining his thirty-five year history of timely filings, including his estimated tax payments for the years in question. He knows there is no way he failed to file for two years in a row. This is just not something that he would ever let happen. He calls the IRS to see if they have received his federal returns and he is told that the IRS has both returns. He orders transcript copies of the federal filings. Now he is more than certain that he filed his New Jersey returns. Luckily, he had filed electronically since 2013.

Dr. Zielinski inquires why the Division of Taxation collected, and spent, the Estimated Taxes he sent each quarter for the years in question, but didn't warn him that he "failed to file a return" for those same years. He was told, "It doesn't work that way."

He receives a piece of mail that he almost discards due to its unofficial looking presentation. He opens it on the way to the recycling bin and finds that his 'tax debt' has been turned over to the Pioneer Credit Recovery, Inc. He is incredulous . . . what an adventurous name for a collections company. He is sure that it is some kind of scam, but it isn't. The State of New Jersey turns such tax situations to private collection agencies. He explains his situation to the assigned collection manager. She is clearly dedicated to one purpose only, collecting the money to obtain her commission. The case manager very calmly states, "I know you think that you probably don't owe anything, but your overpayments can not be credited and the balance is as stated." She pauses, "Unless you can prove that you mailed the returns in when you claim you did, you owe the money."

Dr. Zielinski is adamant, "But the State got the money. This is not a delinquent account. In fact, the Division got some of the money early through the rolled over overpayments each year. This is morally wrong. It seems that my filing record for decades counts for nothing."

The case manager continues, "You can fight it if you want, but interest continues to accrue and you will have to prove that you filed in a timely way. Did you file the returns with a return receipt requested?"

"No . . . Who does that?"

"Some people do."

"But most people don't. Why am I being held to a higher standard?"

"It's up to you how you proceed."

Dr. Zielinski fights to contain himself. "Thank you." He hangs up. He is again unsure of how to move forward. He decides to call the Division. After identifying himself the rep looks up his account.

The tax rep informs him, "Oh, since this is already in collections, we can't speak to you about this matter. You have to speak directly with the collections manager on your account."

He is now furious in his helplessness. "This was still in dispute. How does the State get to do this to an honest taxpayer without notice?"

The rep acts surprised. "You didn't receive any notice?"

"No."

"We have a record that we informed you of this."

Later that day, Dr. Zielinski receives and opens his mail. The notice from the Division that his account has been forwarded to a collections agency is there.

Karen overhears one of his phone calls. Dr. Zielinski is beside himself in fury over the abject unfairness of the situation. He looks at her. "I might as well take six thousand dollars, walk down the hall and flush it. Get out my check book . . . I'll write the checks to minimize the damage until I decide what to do."

Karen is sympathetic. She offers, "From what you've been saying, it looks like they are just out to get you on this."

Something clicks with him. "Karen, get out the letter I sent to the Governor on Kristin's behalf. Let's check the date."

"OK, why?"

They get the letter out. He exclaims, "February 2012, in the same time frame to get both returns pulled. You know me and you know that I file everything on time. How could two years in a row be missing . . . unless someone tampered with it?"

Karen waits hesitantly.

He continues, "I think the letter I wrote for Kristin struck a nerve and they didn't like it. Someone pulled the returns out knowing it would take this long to show up and that the statute would punish me . . . That's what I think."

Dr. Zielinski continues, "OK, I'll write another letter to the Governor, with the same information the Division got, but with the added proviso that I will explore criminal action through the Audit Department, the Division of Law, the State Police . . . anyone I can get. Let's see what happens."

Karen offers, "You're spending a lot of time on this. I don't think you'll get satisfaction."

"You know I have to try. I don't know any other way. Who the hell do they think they are?"

Three weeks go by. Karen takes a phone message from the Division of Taxation. Dr. Zielinski returns it. The division rep answers.

Her tone is actually nervous, extremely apologetic, even solicitous. "Dr. Zielinski, we looked into it further, and it appears that you did file in a timely way. So, we will be returning your money with three separate checks. There will be accounting notices which will precede them. You can expect them shortly." She waits, appearing to be hoping for a positive response, as if there is some possible repercussion if I am unhappy.

Dr. Zielinski involuntarily grins ear-to-ear. Noting her nervousness, and knowing that he will pursue this at a future time, he demurs, "Thank you, thank you very much. This will be great with the holidays coming." They hang up. He is ecstatic in his vindication. It took five months, but his determination paid off.

Dr. Zielinski is convinced that there was illegal activity with regard to his tax returns. He has to decide how he will pursue it. He thinks, "First there was Bridgegate. Now this. Corruption reigns. Why in God's name would they reverse their position like this? Why would this rep be so apologetic and anxious about this?" Over time, he feels the Division of Taxation was involved with someone in government in an unsavory manner. True or not, there have been such accusations in the past.

Chapter 29

A few months go by and I'm able to come see Dr. Zielinski. I catch him up on all that's been happening at home with the baby, and then we talk about work.

"You know how I'm still having Workman's Comp hearings. They sent me to six Independent Medical Exam doctors over the last year or so. But they spent most of the time talking about your letter to the governor, not the doctors' reports. They said I was hiding something with you. They wanted to know why you sent a letter to the Governor," I say.

"If they read the letter, they'd know why I sent it," Dr. Zielinski says sarcastically.

"They want to reduce my compensation by twenty-five percent because of the letter," I say.

"That makes no sense. I don't see logic in that at all, only revenge."

"My lawyer told me their lawyer really dislikes me."

Dr. Zielinski asks me if he can get copies of the Independent Medical Exam reports and I agree without hesitation. He makes several efforts to obtain the IME reports. Even though he executes a HIPAA compliant release form with my signature, it takes him four follow-up phone calls to my attorney over three weeks to get them mailed. He peruses his copies of the six Independent Medical Examinations. To his surprise, they are truly independent in that all of them support my PTSD diagnosis and recommend evidence-based treatment for it. No hired guns are among them. Yet, the State's Workman's Comp decision-makers are blocking my access to Eye Movement Desensitization and Reprocessing, a specific, evidence-based treatment for PTSD that the IMEs recommended, one that Dr. Zielinski has not been trained in. He had been pulled as my Workman's Compensation therapist early in the litigation process and was not a direct factor in this issue save for his letter to the governor. The State pulled me from my treating psychiatrist, Dr. Rosenberg, ostensibly because he was totally supportive of my position and need for ongoing treatment, documenting my needs in an entire letter.

I am forced to see Dr. Nemeroff, and I actually find him empathic and helpful. One Philadelphia psychiatrist, Dr. James Balfour Hoyme, goes above and beyond, reinstating my belief in goodness in the world. He demolishes and baits DCPP in his report and makes strident statements about my situation and my need for treatment. Still, all of these doctors' recommendations, which the State required me to visit, and for which the State paid for, go unheeded. The amount of money they paid for the six evaluations could easily have paid for the treatment. If they authorize the treatment, does it imply liability? Whatever the reason, the State of New Jersey has its own dedicated Workman's Compensation insurance department, giving them total control.

Zielinski contemplates learning and attempting Eye Movement Desensitization and Re-processing (EMDR) with me. He doesn't want me to be his first EMDR patient, but the reality is, there is always a first. He researches it. Originally trained as a behavior therapist, he is keenly aware of how to develop a hierarchy of feared and anxiety provoking event images, as well as how to use relaxation in a desensitization process, called systematic desensitization. He also knows how to use positive imagery. Finally, he knows me and what I have been through.

He also learns that EMDR is without known side effects, so there is little risk, only that it might not work. But the State isn't letting anyone else do it. It makes no sense. It's not a lengthy or expensive treatment. He has been seeing me under my Medicaid insurance and he could implement this treatment within that. Since the State of New Jersey is not sending me for treatment through my Workman's Compensation benefits, despite six doctors' recommendations to do so, the State is not considering my condition to be work related. To do so would be illegal on their part. So, Dr. Zielinski feels justified in proceeding.

Dr. Zielinski explains all that he knows to me. He notes that the theory posits that certain eye movements reduced the intensity of disturbing thoughts. He adds that no one knows why the eye movements actually help, but that they do. The ultimate goal of the treatment is to develop more adaptive coping mechanisms.

I trust Dr. Zielinski, after all I've known him for years now. So when he asks me to be his first patient to try EMDR, I say yes.

Dr. Zielinski and I develop a hierarchy of problematic traumatic and distressing images, as well as my negative cognition associated with the images. This is followed by a positive cognition to be associated with the image that is desired in place of the negative one, as well as a measure of the strength of the positive cognition. I take well to the structure of the treatment and we begin. We begin this on April 1st, 2015, six years and one day after Jamarr's death. I become tearful during the images, but I initially comply with the treatment. However, I avoid starting EMDR in following sessions by bringing up other topics. Dr. Zielinski senses this, but goes along with me. The images are just too painful for me.

Not long after, the State of New Jersey permits Dr. Zielinski to be my "official" Workman's Comp therapist. The order is given by Judge E. Spevak.

Then, the State changes its mind and sends me a letter from Horizon's Casualty Case Manager that I am to see another psychologist, Dr. Jeff Bessey, for my Workman's Compensation treatment. Once again, the State does what it wants, when it wants. Nevertheless, Dr. Zielinski encourages me to follow their directive and notes that this psychologist has training in EMDR. I do follow through, but after a few sessions, Dr. Bessey finds that I am too anxious for him to use the treatment. He states that so much time has passed that I have generalized my anxiety to so many situations beyond the original ones that I simply can't settle down enough to proceed.

The final straw is the latest State position that they want my EEOC settlement to offset two-thirds of my Workman's Compensation settlement. Bargain, bargain, bargain, at my expense. Not only that, but the settlement date is far into 2017. There is no end in sight. At least they backed off of reducing it by twenty-five percent because of Dr. Zielinski's letter to Governor Christie. The State continues to create one subterfuge after another. That is probably the message they want to send: We will drag this out so long and cost you so much, that anyone dare not sue the State of New Jersey for anything, regardless of how just. I dared, and I continue to pay the price.

Chapter 30

After multiple attempts to get some attention from the press, Dr. Zielinski and I speak with several young reporters, some by phone. They take notes and act concerned.

"Well . . . what do you think?" I ask Dr. Zielinski.

"I don't know, I've never done this before. They're all young, which is not a great sign," he says, sounding uncertain.

Days go by. Neither Dr. Zielinski nor I hear anything. Dr. Zielinski is only partly surprised. He tries to call each reporter on the phone, leaving messages. Karen sits at her desk as Dr. Zielinski hangs up the phone. "No one wants to listen. Kristin and I did four interviews . . . four different reporters in two weeks. They took her story, acted interested, and just dropped it. I don't get it."

Dr. Zielinski gets a lead to contact a prominent reporter for the *Philadelphia Inquirer.* He e-mails a cover letter with the back story via an attachment. He waits a few days, then calls her.

She is blunt, abrupt. "I looked up the case. All of the information says that Vince Williams was very clever at hiding the abuse. There is no evidence of any other wrong doing or of any cover ups. There is nothing more to report."

Dr. Zielinski is momentarily taken aback. "But that is what this is all about. That's exactly what my information is about."

"There's nothing there." The reporter ends the conversation and hangs up.

Dr. Zielinski begins to wonder if the press is involved, if they afraid to take on the State.

He calls me about the results, and I am disappointed, but not surprised. Dr. Zielinski shares his frustration with me. "They won't even return my phone calls. How can someone just get away with this?" He pauses. "Maybe we waited too long . . . a stale story?" He later learns that funding issues have left many newspapers without a sturdy investigative team, and they simply might not have the personnel resources to do the research.

Unfortunately, nobody wants to hear my story.

Later that year, I share in therapy that an inside confidant told me that Olivia was maneuvered out of a promotion by Hilda.

I tell Dr. Zielinski what the confidant told me. "Olivia had scored first on the Civil Service Exam in Camden County. The departmental policy is to interview candidates in threes and to pick the best of the top three. Hilda Vega deliberately invited a candidate from another county with a slightly higher score. All three candidates interviewed well, but she gave the promotion to the candidate with the higher score. It was crafty, yet blatant. Hilda was overheard saying, 'How does Olivia like her job? I hope she does, because she's going to be there for a long time.'"

I shake my head. "It's six years later and she's still holding Olivia's honesty over her head. As always, it just goes on and on. No one is over them. The State does whatever it wants."

I also find out from the same confidant that Ellen, the auditor, is being blocked from promotion. At least they're equal opportunity manipulators. My confidant has moved up to a fairly high level over the years since we worked together. Dr. Zielinski surmises that the confidant's power base must be lacking vis-a-vis those calling the shots in my situation. The confidant wishes to remain anonymous, and indicates that she is not in a position to openly come forward, lest she jeopardize her career.

I learn from another inside confidant more information that I had seen for myself in the Gloucester County Office. The numbers were and are manipulated and cases were "assigned" to other people, even supervisors, to make the data appear better than it really was. I was privy to several conversations during my tenure there. A CWA state area director, Ms. Rosenstein, had previously stated that "management has developed a single-minded devotion to meeting the statistics-driven requirements of the settlement (lawsuit) that has trumped casework." Both department leaders and Ms. Meltzer have disputed this contention. However, the numbers are reported to document that DCPP had met its goals and New Jersey was now being offered as a model state for other states to emulate in terms of child protection.

Both public announcements and media presentations touted the State of New Jersey's 'new and improved' child advocacy program. Governor Christie is exploring the feasibility of trying to end the Federal Monitor's purview of DCPP based on the data. The State of New Jersey has met over half of its goals. However, the original settlement required two years of overview after DCPP had met all of its goals. Not all are in favor of dropping the oversight of the monitor, but the fact that the question is being asked raises the possibility.

I wonder how many children are still at risk with this kind of bold faced lying. I know businesses "cook the books," but to manipulate the data and then tout the results to the entire country is brazenly corrupt.

More weeks go by. I contemplate what I will do with the rest of my life. Yes, I have children, including an infant to take care of, but Benny and I, like most families, need two incomes. Should I deliver pizzas? I have never even considered doing anything except working as a child caseworker. I thought I would win. I thought the powers that be would take me back to work. They didn't. I have tried to gain employment, but I have been unsuccessful for reasons that are unclear to me. I am now left to live as a disgraced state worker. Who would even take the time to listen to my story, let alone actually believe it?

I am driving in Camden with my younger children. I make a wrong turn. I am on Jamarr's old street. How did I get here? Was this an unconciously motivated mistake? I pull over and I am in front of his old house. My kids are bewildered as tears stream down my face. I can't speak or explain to them what I am feeling. I worry that Jamarr believed that I abandoned him. I want him to know that I didn't. I tried my best, but I failed to keep my promise. My kids ask, "Mommy, what's wrong?" I have to move on. I can move my car . . . but I have yet to move my life forward.

Postface

Though the local union originally pushed for me to take the punishment deal, and refused to get me representation, a national union representative risked his own job to champion my cause, resulting in getting the two lawyers who helped me to win the arbitration. I was told that my courage and persistence set a precedent for other workers.

Two of my witnesses, Olivia Figueroa and Ellen Finley, are willing to testify about the impropriety of being pressured to alter their testimony when protected by official, impartial investigations. Their names have been changed.

The arbitration records indicate my optimal handling of the entire situation and point to the truly guilty parties.

The State of New Jersey's Attorney General's Office is dedicated to prosecuting criminal acts under their purview. At the same time, it serves in a legal advisory role as "the sole legal advisor" to the State's personnel which includes "legal advice and counsel to the Governor and all departments, boards, and commissions," which includes client-attorney privilege. The fox guards the hen house. The Division of Law's mission statement as quoted from its official website is, among other things, "imbued with the public trust to further the public interest in all matters in which the State is involved." How does one define "public interest?"

The Attorney General's Office has an army of attorneys on their payroll, which allows them to take their time in litigation matters while the plaintiff incurs a loss of income and additional costs. The size and inertia of the Attorney General's Office affords them a strategic position in matters of litigation against small law firms.

There is a pattern in the State of New Jersey of punishing whistle blowers. There also appears to be a sanctioned pattern of favoritism, cronyism, and misguided loyalties that developed over decades leading to complicity, political corruption, and abuse of power that remains unchecked. For example, the agency director at the time of Jamarr's death and my arbitration, Christine Moses, was promoted rather than being investigated.

The Division of Child Protection & Permanency was sued by Omayra Cruz, Jamarr's mother, in 2013, and I was named among other defendants in the suit. A $425,000.00 settlement was accepted by Omayra Cruz from the State of New Jersey and this is readily verifiable in New Jersey's Open Public Records Act. In our view, the settlement was made to avoid a public court trial and public exposure of the facts. Although the rumors have not been substantiated, many sources from DYFS as well as members of the community have stated that Omayra was also paid millions of dollars in hush money, and that the maternal grandparents and Jamarr's birthfather also received money from an unknown source.

There have been multiple conversations about data being shifted within the agency's system, e.g., Gloucester County Office, to make the numbers look more effective, than they, in fact, are. If audited, evidence will surely be revealed to support this malpractice.

Several reporters were approached with my story and no one chose to publish anything in any form, or to investigate further.

The State of New Jersey required my lifetime resignation from DCPP in order to for me to receive the monetary settlement in the EEOC suit. I signed the lifetime resignation and accepted a settlement in 2014 due to the prolonged emotional and financial hardship both on myself and my family. The settlement was for $250,000, which after attorneys' fees and expenses, left me with $125,000. I did not receive full compensation for my back wages. I regret my decision, especially because the resignation bars me from working with any and all vendors and social service agencies that contract with New Jersey's DCPP. Additionally, the State of New Jersey wants to subtract my EEOC award from the Workman's Compensation award.

None of the principals came forward to confess their involvement. This is worthy of further investigation and should be made available to the public. Who are the state's personnel who are the principal stakeholders in the position taken on my firing, ignored arbitration, and forced resignation?

The highly unusual situation of Dr. Zielinski's New Jersey State Tax Returns needs to be investigated. The stonewalling followed by a complete reversal when threatened with litigation is highly suspect.

Dr. Joseph Zielinski and I wrote this book to seek justice for me and to pursue those at fault for Jamarr's death. We aim to expose treachery and conspiracy in the State of New Jersey. A confluence of factors was at work to cause the termination of my career as a child protective services caseworker. My stance in the matter could and should be used as a critical incident training opportunity for child protective services nationwide.

The guilty parties in this bureaucracy need to be exposed, tried in court, and punished according to their level of involvement. Innocent children need to be protected. Case management decisions need to be data driven. Brave individuals who stand up for what is right need to be acknowledged and utilized for their insight and suggestions, not punished. New Jersey's DCPP is being wrongly extolled as a model for the rest of the country. It must first get its own house in order.

Our ultimate goal is for the State of New Jersey's Attorney General's Office to investigate misfeasance, malfeasance, and criminal activity among DCPP state employees.

My now longtime fantasy is to establish and run an exemplary foster facility, even a statewide system, in New Jersey which does justice to the needs of the state's children, to be staffed by top notch providers and professionals.

Kristin I. Morris

Kristin I. Morris is an activist who volunteers her time with organizations for women, children and families, including Toys for Tots, She's Got a Name, and Urban Promise. She has been with her husband Benny since she was nineteen and they have four very active children. She always wanted to help people, by working with the church teaching CCD, pro-life club, soup kitchen, and through charity work.

Kristin earned her bachelor's in Psychology from Rowan University. After school, she began to work for the State of New Jersey's Division of Child Protection and Permanency, formerly Division of Youth and Family Services. She found herself watching over New Jersey's most vulnerable citizens: abused children. She was extremely excited and naïve, wanting to save the world. Working in the city of Camden among the people that needed the most help was extremely eye opening, but most alarming was how the inner systems of the Division worked. *Jamarr's Promise* is the true story of Kristin's battle with the State over the murder of a child she tried desperately to save.

Kristin's dream is to open and run a foster care organization as a safety net for abused children, and to eliminate the politics and hidden agendas of larger organizations.

Joseph J. Zielinski, Ph.D.

Joseph J. Zielinski, Ph.D. is a New Jersey licensed psychologist board certified in both Clinical Psychology and Clinical Neuropsychology. He completed his undergraduate in Psychology at the University of Pennsylvania and earned a Ph.D. in Clinical Psychology at Rutgers University, New Brunswick. He has been in private practice for forty years as a psychologist, often working concurrently for public schools in special education, in a headache clinic, and in a management consulting firm. He has published in professional journals. He most enjoys working as a practitioner and seeing patients of all backgrounds and experiences.

For seventeen years, Dr. Zielinski has spearheaded the Committee for Prescriptive Authority, a group of pioneering psychologists, to pass legislation allowing trained psychologists to prescribe psychotropic medications. This is an effort to help the dire shortage of psychiatrists in New Jersey and around the country. Their efforts to help the people of New Jersey are near to fruition.

Dr. Zielinski has been married for forty years, has two grown children and two grandchildren. He is an avid landscaper and is particularly fond of evergreens. He is a fitness enthusiast and a former marathoner. He enjoys classic rock and live concerts at local venues and attending professional sporting events with his daughter. He enjoys writing screenplays and has pitched a few to Hollywood professionals.

change.org

Seeking Justice for Caseworker who warned NJ DYFS before Tragic Death of 9-Year-Old Boy

Jamarr's Promise is the shocking true story of Kristin I. Morris' fight to protect a nine-year-old child, Jamarr Cruz, that ended in his tragic death and New Jersey's Division of Youth and Family Services (DYFS)'s denial of its responsibility in the case.

As a caseworker for New Jersey's Division of Youth and Family Services (DYFS), Kristin helped many children and families; it was her life's passion. Nine-year-old Jamarr was living with his grandparents after his mother's boyfriend, Vincent Williams, beat him. During the last required monthly visit before Jamarr was scheduled to return to his mother and Vincent's care, Jamarr told Kristin it was not safe for him to return home. **Kristin urgently tried to keep Jamarr safe with his grandparents, but was told by superiors that Latino children are kept in the home at all costs.** This time, the cost was Jamarr Cruz's life.

In 2009 after his return to Omayra Cruz and Vincent Williams, Vincent beat Jamarr to death. **Not only did Kristin's superiors at the DYFS block her efforts to help Jamarr, but when he was killed, they blamed Kristin for his death.** Kristin was terminated at work and sued by Jamarr's mother Omayra Cruz—even after Omayra won a settlement for $425,000 from the State of New Jersey. Kristin's witnesses who provided proof of Kristin's innocence were pressured to alter their testimony by Kristin's superiors. After Kristin won a court arbitration, was completely exonerated, and was ordered to be permitted back at work, DYFS still would not let Kristin return to work. **Meanwhile, those above Kristin who sealed Jamarr's cruel fate have been promoted to higher offices.**

The State of New Jersey has crippled Kristin financially, has stripped her of a career helping vulnerable children, and has blatantly ignored facts and sworn testimonies that an investigation of the herein named DYFS and State corroborators is necessary. **Jamarr's Promise is a call to end corrupt loyalties in New Jersey's DYFS.** It is a call to protect children from Jamarr's fate. It is a call for justice for Kristin Morris, who did the right thing and was punished unjustly for it.

Sign our petition here at Change.org and call for a full investigation of those responsible for the mismanagement of the Jamarr Cruz case, from Joyce A. Thomas, NY/NJ Regional Administrator of the Administration for Children & Families.

Petitioning Joyce.Thomas@acf.hhs.gov

https://goo.gl/YKWzUq

CPSIA information can be obtained
at www.ICGtesting.com
Printed in the USA
BVOW04s2202110517
483890BV00001B/4/P